Mixed Power and Missiles

By the end of 1956 the MiG OKB had a clear idea how they would proceed in developing the selected light frontal fighter, the delta-winged MiG-21. In parallel, they continued to work on a mixed-power (turbojet-plus-rocket) interceptor which had occupied the attention of part of the project staff since mid-1954. This was the Ye-50, already mentioned.

In 1946-48 the OKB had designed and flown two prototypes of Aircraft J (I-270), a short-range interceptor powered solely by a twin-chamber rocket engine. Now, in parallel with the light fighter programme, it was gaining extensive experience testing larger supersonic fighters with booster rockets added underneath, but it had not flown a true mixed-power

---

The Ye-50-3 was painted pale grey overall. Like the Ye-2 family, the ailerons were in two sections, inner and outer. Yefim Gordon archive

aircraft with a pilot-controllable rocket engine permanently installed. It had been intensely interested to learn of the British Saunders-Roe SR.53 and SR.177, which appeared likely to be an outstanding aircraft. Moreover, at the start of work on the light frontal fighter, the fact that the desired engine, the AM-11, was not going to be available for at least a year prompted the launch of a project to match the lower-powered engine that was immediately available with a rocket engine. This was given the MiG OKB designation Ye-50.

The airframe was originally to be that of the Ye-1, but it ended up based on that of the Ye-2A. Compared with that aircraft, the main differences concerned the tankage, and the aft fuselage behind Frame No.28A, which was completely new. The main engine was the AM-9Ye, by 1956 called the RD-9Ye, fed from a group of kerosene tanks in the modified tank bays in the centre fuselage.

The rocket engine was the S-155 developed by the KB of L S Dushkin, with a single thrust chamber having a maximum rating of 1,300kg (2,866lb) at sea level and about 1,600kg (3,527lb) at high altitude. It was installed in a fireproof rear fuselage bay added at the base of the fin and rudder, which had the effect of considerably increasing the area of the vertical tail. It was fed from a group of three tanks housing concentrated nitric acid, high-test hydrogen peroxide (HTP) and compressed nitrogen for purging, feeding the propellants and starting the engine. The HTP tank was in the fin, and this highly reactive liquid also drove the rocket-engine turbopump which was installed under the front of the fin together with the complex control system. Special materials and coatings were needed throughout the rocket engine bay and tankage to guard against any spillage of acid or HTP.

Feed pipes were run in external fairings

along the sides of the fuselage ahead of the fixed roots of the tailplanes. The greater fin area made it possible to replace the canted ventral strakes by shallow fairings over the two stainless-steel pipes used for dumping, draining and purging the propellant system.

Eventually the OKB received funding for three Ye-50 aircraft, each to be assigned to a pilot from one of the LII State flight-research institutes at Zhukovskii. The Ye-50-1 was completed in late 1955 with normal instruments and electronics for flight test, such as RSIU-3M, ARK-5 and MRP-48P, but without military equipment, such as guns, gunsight, RWR or IFF. The

pilot assigned to it was Valentin G Mukhin, from the LII-MAP, who opened the flight test programme, using the turbojet alone, on 9th January 1956. The first flight cleared to fire the rocket engine was on 8th June 1956, when it was operated for eleven seconds at an altitude of 9km (5.6 miles). Unfortunately, at the conclusion of the 18th flight, on 14th July, the Ye-50-1 made a heavy landing short of the runway, and was damaged beyond repair.

The Ye-50-2 differed in having the lower portion of the rudder transferred to the fin below its base; at the same time, a sharp edged strip was added at the rudder's trailing edge to increase

chord. Another major difference was that this aircraft was fully equipped as a fighter, with two NR-30 guns, Grad ('Hail') radar ranging sight and Barii-M IFF, but surprisingly without the Sirena-2 RWR. It also had a duplicate VHF antenna under the fuselage and a duplicate PVD air-data boom on the right wing tip. This aircraft was the only one of the MiG light fighter prototypes to be painted, the colour believed to have been battleship grey.

The pilot assigned to the Ye-50-2 was Valentin P Vasin, also from the LII-MAP. He had two main causes for concern. The loaded weight had risen to above 8,500kg (18,739lb), which made take-offs, using only the low powered turbojet, require almost the entire Zhukovskii runway, and the very limited kerosene capacity limited range to below 450km (280 miles). On an early (but not the first) flight, on 17th June 1957, he climbed to high altitude and then fired the S-155 to dry tanks in a maximum performance test which reached 2,460km/h (1,529 mph, about Mach 2.32) and a height of 25.6km (15.9 miles). Here Vasin encountered trouble with the new VKK-6 design of pressurised flight suit and 'bone-dome'. On another flight he became the first pilot to fire the S-155 at the start of take-off, thereafter reaching 10km (6.2 miles) in 6.7 minutes (not an impressive figure) and 20km (12.4 miles) in 9.4 minutes.

The third aircraft, the Ye-50-3, had a redesigned nose section, extended by 0.395m (15.6in). This lengthened the fuselage from 12.32 to 12.715m (40ft 3in to 41ft 6½in), but – though all other parts of the aircraft appear to have been unchanged – available records show that the overall length, excluding the PVD, was 14.85m (48ft 6½in). This is puzzling, and the figure measured off drawings is 14.02m (45ft 8½in), which tallies with the extra length of nose. The new nose incorporated a more efficient conical centre-body of Oswatitsch double-shock type, focusing two oblique shocks and one normal shock on the sharp peripheral lip, giving improved pressure recovery at high supersonic Mach numbers. For best efficiency the cone was arranged to translate (move axially), sliding in and out according to Mach number, the control system necessitating a small

fairing above the nose. This principle was to be a feature of all production MiG-21s.

A further modification in the Ye-50-3 was a reduction in the HTP tankage and replacement of a flexible kerosene tank by a larger integral tank and transfer pump. This was expected to increase range by some 200km (124 miles). The pilot assigned to this aircraft was N A Korovin, from the NII-VVS. On one of his first flights, in autumn 1957, the S-155 malfunctioned catastrophically. One report says that a prolonged fire destroyed the tail control linkages, while another says that an explosion virtually blew the tail off. In either event Korovin had to eject, but was tragically killed.

On the whole the Ye-50 had performed well up to expectations, and the mixed-power formula appeared to be likely to result in a superior high altitude interceptor. In 1956, before the Ye-50-3 had flown, the MiG OKB had proposed various improved versions, most of them based on the airframe of the Ye-2A/Ye-5 with the RD-11 engine. This fuselage was considerably shorter than that of any of the Ye-50s, and drastic action was needed to accommodate the required quantity of kerosene and rocket propellants. The obvious answer was to scab on an additional tank underneath.

At this point it should be noted that the MiG OKB were, of course, well aware of the Area Rule. This decrees that, for minimum wave drag, a high speed aircraft should be so designed that the plot of total cross sectional areas – the areas of transverse slices cut through the entire aircraft – should form a smooth curve from nose to tail. Thus, adding area in one region (such as a canopy or wing) should be countered by either waisting the adjacent fuselage or by bulging the fuselage ahead of and behind the added part. The rule is modified for supersonic aircraft to take account of the fact that, as Mach number increases, the shock waves lean back at an increasing angle. From the start the MiG lightweight prototypes were well matched to the rule, because the wing volume was small, it began as the canopy tapered off, and was distributed over a considerable length of the aircraft. Adding the giant central tank could be made to conform approximately to the rule, merely enlarging the area under the plotted curve of cross-sections.

Tunnel testing of a model suggested that drag would not be increased very much, and the OKB therefore went ahead and built a mock-up which was quickly approved. Gorkii

was given a contract to build a single prototype designated Ye-50A. It was expected that this aircraft, in a refined form, would go into production as the MiG-23U (U signifying not Uchyebnii, trainer, but Uskoritel, literally: accelerated). The OKB designation was Type 64.

Compared with the Ye-2A the forward fuselage (back to Frame No.20) and wing were identical, though the main wheels were altered to match the increased take-off weight. Curiously, though the obvious way to alter the wheels would have been to make them larger, neither surviving drawings nor artwork shows blisters caused by the retracted wheels, though

this was a feature of the much lighter pre-series MiG-23 aircraft. At the rear, two of the seven kerosene tanks were removed, though the installation of the S-155 was almost the same as before. The very large circular section ventral tank was divided into compartments housing the HTP, nitric acid and the rocket control system. It was arranged so that it could quickly be removed (though not jettisoned in flight), and its presence required the addition of two large diagonal under-fins at the tail. Compared with the Ye-2A the wheelbase was unchanged, despite the slight increase in fuselage length from 11.33 to 11.53m (37ft 1in to 37ft 7in).

The Ye-50-3 had a longer nose, modified tail, revised rocket installation and no ventral radio antenna. Yefim Gordon archive

Overhead view of the Ye-50-3, showing that the fairings ahead of the tailplane roots were also aerodynamic strakes. The Ye-50s had no main wheel blisters. Yefim Gordon archive

While the Ye-50A was being built, in 1957, Gorkii was given the expected initial order for two series MiG-23Us (Type 64). In the event it was all to come to nothing. After prolonged testing with several other MiG prototypes (including service experience with the SM-51 and SM-52) and the Yak-27V, and planned tests with a mixed-power Sukhoi T-43, it was decided at Minister level that rocket engines were not the way to go. Tumanskii's confident prediction of more powerful lightweight turbojets influenced this decision. Another factor may have been Britain's cancellation of the SR.177 in April 1957, though that had nothing whatsoever to do with the aircraft itself but reflected the Ministerial belief that fighters were obsolete as a class! The Dushkin KB was promptly closed, leaving the Ye-50A programme in limbo, with the prototype incomplete.

This left the light fighter programme with propulsion solely by an afterburning turbojet, which Mikoyan himself tended to welcome. Tumanskii's team had worked around the clock both to improve the maturity of the RD-11 and to produce improved versions, and over the longer term he succeeded with both. As had happened with the single-spool engines, as used in the MiG-19, the relentless drive of Tumanskii and, from 1973, his successors Gavrilov and Khachaturov, was to result in a succession of ever better engines over 25 years that were instrumental in keeping the MiG-21 competitive.

By 1957, as a result of intensive testing of the experimental Type 37F turbojets, Tumanskii could offer an improved engine, the R-11F-300. This retained almost the same gas generator (compressor, combustion chamber and turbine) but featured an improved afterburner, enabling maximum dry and reheat ratings to be established at 3,880 and 5,740kg (8,554 and 12,654lb) respectively. This was available for the next group of three light delta prototypes constructed in 1957-58, designated Ye-6. These were regarded as pre-production aircraft, built under chief engineer I I Rotchik, assisted by the major involvement of Minayev's systems laboratory.

The first of this family, the Ye-6/1, had a wing based upon that of the Ye-5, but with the tips removed, giving a span reduced to 7.154m (23ft 5⅝in). Wing chord was increased at the rear, the ailerons were reduced in span (stopping further from the tip), and each wing was fitted with a hardpoint for a pylon. At the root the fuselage attachment rib was extended in front of the wing, as on the swept-wing prototypes but not behind the trailing edge.

The rear fuselage and tail showed several modifications. The tail end of the fuselage was considerably enlarged in both diameter and length, which gave the final aerodynamic improvement needed. The horizontal tail was moved to the rear to oversail the new nozzle, and also moved down to the mid-level and mounted horizontally instead of having anhedral, so that each tip stayed in the original place. The fixed portion at the root of each tailplane was almost eliminated, but the tailplanes themselves were enlarged to retain the span at 3.74m (12ft 2in). The engine bay cooling inlets were left where they were, now isolated above the tailplanes, and moving the tailplanes down also resulted in blisters directly behind the cooling inlets caused by the tailplane actuating arms. The vertical tail was slightly increased in area, and the fin was joined to the spine by a dorsal fin incorporating the q-feel ram inlet. The curved diagonal ventral strakes were replaced by a single large underfin on the centre-line, the leading edge of which formed a dielectric antenna. Immediately above this a bay in the left side of the fuselage housed a circular braking parachute, connected by cable to an anchor under the rear part of the under-fin.

The nose inlet was redesigned, the sharp outer lip being slightly inclined in side view to improve pressure recovery at high AoA. The conical centre-body was arranged to slide axially to any of three positions. The canopy was a refined version of that tested on the Ye-2A/6. To prevent a repetition of the failure that killed Korovin, the rear arched frame was made even stronger, with two blister fairings over the seat thrust pivots, and the fixed rear portion was also modified to have a stronger frame. The lower tailplanes in turn required that the front pair of airbrakes should be moved forward and changed in shape. Finally, almost all the equipment carried was production, not experimental. One item was a telemetry transmitter for air data and flight test figures, the antenna being on the underside of the fuselage immediately behind the compartment for the nose gear.

The Ye-6/1 was ready for factory testing in May 1958, and in the same month the Ye-4 and Ye-5 prototypes finished a comprehensive series of tests to establish the optimum aerodynamics of supersonic delta-wing fighters. The Ye-4 had flown over 100 times exploring behaviour up to Mach 1.45, including spinning. In a further 98 flights the Ye-5 had taken the testing up to Mach 1.85 at 18km (59.055ft). The various Ye-2 and Ye-2A prototypes had added a further 250 flights.

The flight development of the Ye-6 family opened on 20th May 1958, when Ye-6/1 was flown from LII-MAP at Zhukovskii by Nefyedov. From the start it proved to be an excellent aircraft, immediately establishing a level Mach number of 2.05 at 12,050m (39,500ft), equivalent to about 2,181km/h (1,355mph). Sadly, this aircraft had a short life. On the seventh flight, on 28th May, the engine suffered a flame-out at about 18km (11.2 miles) high. Nefyedov tried to restart and failed. He was eventually commanded by radio to eject, but he was determined to save the aircraft and its valuable instrumentation record. He continued trying to restart the engine as he neared Zhukovskii, but the Ye-6/1 had only a single hydraulic system, backed up by an emergency electrically driven pump, switched in automatically on battery power should hydraulic pressure fall to a dangerous level.

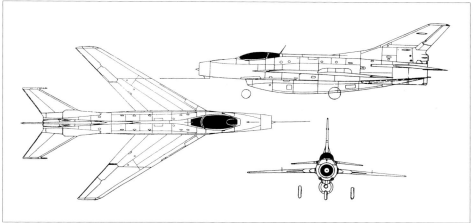

Artist's impression of the unbuilt Ye-50A, produced by retouching a familiar picture of the Ye-2. I Sultanov archive

General arrangement of the unbuilt Ye-50A. Bill Gunston

Apart from the three fences on each wing and the telemetry antenna behind the nose landing gear the Ye-6/1 looked almost identical to the first series MiG-21. The pilot is almost certainly V A Nefyedov. Note the slightly sloping lip round the nose inlet, and the large central under-fin. Yefim Gordon archive

The emergency electric pump was eventually switched in, but too late to prevent Nefyedov losing both lateral and longitudinal control on the final approach. The Ye-6/1 crashed inverted, its pilot dying in hospital of severe burns.

This was a great blow to the LII and to the whole MiG OKB. By this time the Ye-6/2 (call-sign '22') was almost complete. A G Brunov proposed an improvement to the standby electric system, but Rostislav A Belyakov – then deputy chief designer and since 1971 General Director of the Mikoyan bureau – forcefully proposed throwing out the electric standby pump and installing duplicated hydraulics throughout, and Mikoyan accepted this.

The Ye-6/2 was torn apart, extensively reworked and finally flown by Konstantin K Kokkinaki – a senior MiG test pilot and brother of the Ilyushin chief test pilot – on 15th September 1958 with a fully redundant hydraulic system. After completing 15 test flights at Zhukovskii the Ye-6/2 was relocated at Krasnovodsk, on the Caspian shore opposite Baku, to avoid the severe winter. Altogether the Ye-6/2 made 46 flights, whilst having three engine changes (a great improvement on the first RD-11 engines!).

The Ye-6/2 introduced a cleaner wing. The three fences were all removed, satisfactory isobars (equal-pressure lines, showing the airflow at different AoA) being obtained merely by a single very small fence in the same location as the outermost of the original three. On each side of the nose a rectangular auxiliary air inlet was added, to help prevent compressor stalls, as described in the next chapter. Operative NR-30 guns were installed, but with the magazine capacity reduced to 30 rounds each. The principal weapon for the wing pylons was the UB-16-57U launcher for 16 S-5m (ARS-57M) air-ground rockets. Alternative loads included single ARS-240 rockets, or bombs from FAB-50 to FAB-500 (the number referring to weight in kilograms) or napalm tanks.

The third aircraft, the Ye-6/3, call-sign '23', made its first flight in December 1958, and was likewise based at Krasnovodsk. This aircraft introduced a pair of auxiliary engine air inlets, in this case almost square in shape and located immediately below the tapered front end of the wing root rib. It was also the first of the family to have yaw vanes on the PVD, and the first to be fitted with the SRO-2 (Khrom, 'chromium', family) IFF transponder, with antennae beside the nose leg and on top of the fin.

The Ye-6/3 was also the first to test the centre-line tank, mounted on a single shallow pylon. This tank extended the range at high altitude from about 1,400 to 1,800km (870 to 1,118 miles). Other test figures included a level speed of 2,100km/h (1,305 mph, Mach 1.974) at 15.3km (50,200ft), the time to accelerate to this speed at this height from Mach 1.24 being 160 seconds, a service ceiling of 20.7km (67,915ft) with afterburner and 14.5km (47,570ft) in maximum dry power, and the time taken to climb

K K Kokkinaki's Ye-6/2 was later modified with unique wing with a kinked leading edge to give a tip broad enough to carry APU-13 rail launchers for K-13 missiles.
Yefim Gordon archive

from sea level to the ceiling in afterburner being 505 seconds (8 min 25 seconds).

The Ye-6/2 and /3 completed OKB testing in 61 flights. At the conclusion, Kokkinaki reported that a series MiG-21 could be 'flown by any normal pilot, not only by special men'. The recommended never exceed Mach number was set at 2.05. In every flight regime and configuration the stability, control and all round manoeuvrability were judged excellent. Accordingly the Council of Ministers decided to put the aircraft into series production at two factories, No.21 at Gorkii for the VVS and, later, for export customers, at MMZ Znamya Truda (Banner of Labour), the former factory No.30, in Moscow.

While the Ye-6/2 and /3 were beginning their flight test programmes in the fourth quarter of 1958 the MiG OKB was informed that a new short range air-to-air missile was being developed. A particular feature of this weapon was that it would be readily amenable to being fired from fighters with a minimum of special onboard equipment. This missile was a copy of the American AIM-9 Sidewinder.

in the first part of 1962, when it was terminated and replaced by the substantially different MiG-21PF. Another of the modifications introduced at aircraft No.74210814 (reported to have been the 115th aircraft) in 1960 was to extend the leading edge of the fin forwards, with a sharp vee profile, to increase area of the vertical tail to 4.08m² (43ft²). Yaw (directional) stability had never been a serious problem, except that any departure from the aircraft travelling in exactly the direction it was pointing had frequently resulted in severe engine malfunction, in particular violent compressor stall and even reversal of airflow in the inlet duct. Little could be done about this problem in the vertical plane, encountered when 'pulling g' in dive pullouts or mock combat, but the larger fin significantly reduced excursions in yaw. Even with pilots aware of the problem, and careful not to yaw the aircraft, the problem persisted. Later versions were to have still larger fins, and 20 years later the Kiev VVS Institute was to test a completely redesigned inlet. (See Chapter 13.)

The second factory, *Znamya Truda*, began delivering export aircraft in the summer of 1960. These were initially delivered to Egypt, Cuba, India, China, Finland, Poland, East Germany (DDR), Czechoslovakia, Hungary, Iraq and Indonesia. Czechoslovakia worked closely with the MiG design bureau, and had no major problem in tooling up the Aero Vodochody National Corporation at Prague-Vodochody to produce a version with the local designation of S-106. The first few Czech-built aircraft were almost identical to the standard MiG-21F-13, but in the remainder the transparent fairing behind the canopy was replaced by a metal panel. The transparency did not significantly improve rearward vision, and it was likewise deleted from all subsequent Soviet versions.

In early 1961 a licence for the MiG-21F-13 and its R-11F-300 engine was sold to The People's Republic of China. Two pattern aircraft and some component knocked down (CKD) kits were delivered, but the programme was almost immediately disrupted by the cultural split between the two countries. Most of the technical documentation was never delivered, and the engine factory at Shenyang reported that 1,097 of the documents they did receive 'contained errors or omissions'. Much later Mr

The Ye-6V/2 had a large parabrake under the rudder, and a sprung tailwheel which is here seen extended, as is the rear airbrake.

The Ye-6V/2 with take-off rockets, centre-line tank and K-13 missiles, but airbrake and tailwheel retracted.

Close-up of Ye-6V/2 with tank, missiles and SU-1500 take-off rockets.

An early production MiG-21F-13, with APU-13 missile launchers and a single NR-30 gun on the right side. All Yefim Gordon archive

Belyakov said to Bill Gunston 'It is ridiculous to imagine that we would waste our time introducing mistakes to our own drawings'.

Chinese development of the resulting J-7 and subsequent versions is covered in Chapter 11. This proceeded completely independently of the Soviet Union.

The rebuilding in 1960 of the Ye-6/2 prototype has already been described in Chapter 3. In the same year the later Ye-6T/1, call-sign 'Red 31', was subjected to a much more extensive rebuild. Part of the modification was to increase internal fuel capacity, and this was to be a feature of the next family of series aircraft. Other changes were with the sole objective of achieving the highest possible flight performance for gaining world records. For homolo-

gation of these records the rebuilt aircraft was given the designation Ye-66A.

To the MiG-21 programme overall, the most important modification in the Ye-66A was to add a fuel tank of 170 litres (37.4 gallons) capacity in the top of the fuselage a short distance behind the cockpit, located between Frames No.14/17. The canopy was slightly modified by being raised at the rear to fair smoothly into a new all-metal aft fairing which tapered much more gradually to rejoin the original spine close to the mid-point of the aircraft, at which point the VHF radio antenna mast was relocated. This considerably changed the aircraft's appearance in the first of a series of steps which eventually changed the narrow spine into a full-length series of large saddle

Three missile-armed MiG-21F-13s, numbers '04', '28' and '40', took part in the Tushino Aviation Day on 9th July 1961. Until this show Western analysts believed the MiG-21 to be the swept-wing 'Faceplate'.

Rocket-assisted take-off by the Ye-6V/2 at the 1961 Tushino show.

Air-to-air picture of a MiG-21F-13. The black smoke is coming from a small container under the right wing. This may be a smoke-generator, but it looks like an ARS-57 rocket launcher.
All Yefim Gordon archive

Removing the seat for servicing from a MiG-21F-13 of the *Polskie Wojska Lotnicze* (PWL – Polish Air Force). Parked MiG-21s seldom have the rudder centred. WAF

Preserved CS-106 of the markings of the *Ceskoslovenské Letectvo* (CL – Czechoslovak Air Force). Czech industry made 194.
Russian Aviation Research Trust

tanks. Tunnel testing of models showed little increase in drag, and this initial increase in volume ahead of most of the wing improved area ruling. The change was to be a feature of the next production version, the MiG-21PF.

To break records simply required brute thrust. Without modifying the inlet and duct, the engine was changed to the R-11F2-300, which, like the extra tank, was to be a feature of the next series version. Maximum airflow was increased to 65kg (143lb) per second, giving maximum dry and afterburning ratings of 3,950 and 6,120kg (8,710 and 13,490lb) respectively. Underneath this already more powerful aircraft was attached an external booster rocket similar in principle to those used on several mixed-power experimental MiG aircraft of the SM fami-

ly. Called a U-21, the demountable package comprised a Dushkin S-3-20M5A rocket engine, with its nozzle inclined 8° downwards, together with its tanks for red fuming nitric acid and HTP propellants and the control system. Installation was assisted by the Central Institute of Aviation Motors, the Dushkin bureau being by this time closed.

The pointed-nose rocket pack was not scabbed on, but was mounted on a shallow pylon extending along almost its full length, attached to aircraft Frames Nos.16 and 28 (the last in the main section of fuselage). These frames and other parts of the fuselage were structurally reinforced.

Gross thrust of both engines together was reported as varying from 11.7-12.07 tonnes

their inherent longitudinal stability. This could be done, for example, by moving the centre of gravity to the rear, or by adding a destabilising canard on the front. Following preliminary model testing in high speed tunnels, the Ye-6T/3 was given small canard surfaces of delta shape with leading-edge angle 45° and cropped tips, and with long forward-pointing mass balance and anti-flutter masses at mid-span. Each surface was freely pivoted about an axis skewed (swept) at 40°, to adopt an angle of incidence aligned with the local airflow. This was the first supersonic canard-equipped aircraft in the USSR. Results were disappointing, but a similar scheme with modified features was flown later on the Ye-8 (Chapter 10).

After its test programme to establish the effectiveness of pivoted canards, the Ye-6T/3 was used as a testbed for the physical (as distinct from electronic) launch systems for guided missiles. From the start it was fitted with APU-13 rails, and several other patterns were tested subsequently.

In the late 1950s many air forces became aware of the fact that in any war with a major power their air bases might be wiped off the map by missiles. Both NATO and the Soviet Union studied jet-lift V/STOL (vertical or short take-off and landing) as a means of dispersing away from such vulnerable bases. The MiG-21 was the exact opposite of the V/STOL class, but from late 1960 special attention was paid to what could be done to enable this increasingly important fighter to operate from short unprepared strips. Later this research was to lead to the jet-lift 23-31 (MiG-21PD) and also to a link with the future MiG-23, the 23-01 (often incorrectly called the MiG-23PD). For the moment the OKB studied less-radical modifications, partly to reduce take-off and landing distance and partly to improve the MiG-21's ability to operate from ice and snow on skis.

The VVS had issued a requirement that all fighters – as distinct from large radar-equipped interceptors – were to be tested on rough

(25,794-26,609lb). This must be erroneous, because the S-3 series engines had a sea level rating of 3 tonnes (6,614lb), rising to about 3.7 tonnes (8,150lb) at high altitude, giving a maximum combined thrust of about 9,820kg (21,650lb). For obvious reasons the central ventral fin was removed and replaced by twin canted fins, each shorter but even deeper (410mm/16in) than the original, their combined area being 2.65m² (28.5ft²). Another change was to sharpen the fin leading edge still further, increasing area to 4.44m² (47.7ft²).

The rebuilt aircraft retained its 'Red 31' call-sign. On 28th April 1961 Mosolov took it in a zoom climb to its dynamic ceiling at 34,714m (113,891ft), to set a new record for absolute altitude. As had been done with previous Soviet records, in the submission to the FAI the loca-tion was given as 'Podmoskovnoye' (this should have been spelt Podmoskovnyi). Western reports translated this as 'Podmoskovnoye aerodrome', not realising that the word merely meant 'in the Moscow district'. The actual airfield was, of course, LII-MAP Zhukovskii. This record stood for 12 years until it was beaten by another OKB pilot, A V Fedotov, flying a MiG Ye-155 prototype, which was reported to the FAI as the Ye-266.

While the Ye-6T/2 was fitted with new wings (Chapter 3), the Ye-6T/3 was the first of several MiG experimental aircraft to be fitted with canards – foreplanes mounted on the forward part of the fuselage. Both the MiG OKB and CAHI had long believed that the manoeuvrability of fighters could possibly be enhanced, without making the aircraft dangerous, by reducing

unpaved airstrips and from snow. This was a severe requirement, and though a little cine film exists of some of these trials no photographs have been discovered. Several design bureaux took part, but none succeeded in designing a good ski system which was also retractable.

There were two chief shapes of ski tested. The first tests, between May and July 1960, were made with the Ye-5/2. Prolonged ground testing gave patchy results, directional stability being poor. Flight tests followed, and though the aircraft remained undamaged the tricky nature of these trials, and the difficulty of designing for retracted skis, led to a switch to a simpler KL (wheel/ski) gear. Even this did not go into service (though it was a feature of series versions of the Sukhoi Su-7B) and the MiG-21 remained tied to paved runways.

The KL was tested on the Ye-6V/1. This aircraft was the first of two Gorkii-built Type 74 (MiG-21F-13) fighters, with the increased chord fin, which were specially modified for STOL testing, receiving the designation Ye-6V. By far the most extensive modification was to fit SPS blown flaps, as described in the next chapter, but for the initial series of trials this system was inoperative. To reduce take-off distance, the fuselage was modified for the attachment of two *uskoritel* (accelerator) rockets. These were of a standard production type, the SU-1500, with a solid filling and a nozzle canted downwards and outwards, giving an average thrust of 3.5 tonnes for 10 seconds. They were attached at Frame No.25, with thrust transmitted through a link to Frame No.28. Results were impressive, and at the Aviation Day show on

9th July 1961 Fedotov was airborne in the Ye-6V/2 in an estimated 200m (656ft). A photograph taken near the start of the run on this occasion shows the tailplanes at their maximum negative angle, to raise the aircraft's nose as quickly as possible. A number of MiG-21F-13 fighters tested this technique in VVS service. Reducing the landing run required more thought. The three wheel brakes were already close to the limit of their effectiveness. Apart from blown flaps, the main effort was directed towards a high angle-of-attack approach and to increasing the drag of the parabrake 'chute. Both of the Ye-6V aircraft were fitted with two parabrake 'chutes. One housed in the normal position and the other placed in an entirely new location in a tube immediately below the rudder.

It was not intended to stream both 'chutes together, but to compare the results obtained with each. It was found that the higher position enabled the 'chute to be streamed before touchdown, resulting in a shorter run. Subsequently the higher location, above the jet pipe, was made standard. The Ye-6V/1 was later used to test different designs of canopy.

The high-AoA testing put all the onus on the pilot. In line service, the VVS recommended making the landing approach at an AoA of 10°-11°, but in Ye-6V testing the angle was set at 16°-18°. On some landings the flaps were locked fully down. To protect the ventral fin it was fitted with a retractable spring-loaded solid-tyred tailwheel. These nose-high landings did not take place until July-August 1963, by which time several further MiG-21 versions had reached the production stage. The pilots found the technique difficult, and potentially dangerous, because throughout the approach they were completely unable to see the runway, and after landing they had poor directional stability. The VVS concluded that, even with special training, this was an unacceptable technique, and that the better answer was to make normal approaches but with blown flaps.

Above: **MiG-21F-13 534 of the Iraqi Air Force, defected to Israel on 16th August 1966. It was evaluated by the *Chel Ha'Avir*, Israeli Defence Force – Air Force, who could not resist giving it the code number '007' for flight tests!**
Russian Aviation Research Trust

Below, left: **A typical Chinese propaganda picture of J-7I (MiG-21F-13) fighters of the People's Liberation Army Air Force. Note the hinged arm over the seat, adjusted for pilot height, which is pushed down by the canopy.**
Yefim Gordon archive

Below right: **Cine film frame taken in the 1970s of the first MiG-21 to join the US Air Force, at Nellis Air Force Base, Nevada.** via Jay Miller

Interceptors

Though the MiG-21F-13 fully met the original 1953 demand for an agile day air-combat fighter with superior flight performance, it was obviously limited in its operational capability. In particular, it had no radar, except for the simple SRD-5M element of the gunsight. This was intended only for the measurement of the range to close targets, to assist accurate gun aiming and to supply target distance to K-13 missiles. This made the MiG-21 useless for the *Istrebitel'naya Aviatsia–Protivovozdusdushnoi Oborony* (IA-PVO – Interceptor Force of the Air Force of the Anti-Aircraft Defence of the Homeland), the fighter element of the Soviet air-defence forces, which had to be able to find and shoot down hostile aircraft at any time, in any weather.

The IA-PVO had to defend the world's largest country, with a frontier 15,850km (9,850 miles) long. Such a gigantic task was, of course, impossible to fulfil completely within any reasonable budget. Only limited numbers of giant long range interceptors – such as the Yakovlev Yak-28P 'Brewer', Sukhoi Su-15 'Flagon', Tupolev Tu-128 'Fiddler' and Mikoyan MiG-25P 'Foxbat' and MiG-31 'Foxhound' – could be afforded. An interceptor version of the MiG-21 was from the outset seen as desirable in order to improve defences of the many important regions close to particularly threatened parts of the frontier, such as in the extreme West.

The obvious answer was to investigate the possibility of fitting the MiG-21 with an effective search radar. During the Second World War pioneer centimetric-wavelength radars had been used successfully in such small fighters as the US Navy Chance Vought Corsair and Grumman Hellcat and the Royal Navy Fairey Firefly. In the Soviet Union by the mid-1950s there was no shortage of airborne radar programmes. Several radar KBs had produced installations suitable for small jet fighters, the most important family being the *Sapfir* (Sap-

phire) series. By early 1957 the RP-9U radar from this family was in series production, and by late 1958 it was in PVO service in the Su-9. This aircraft was similar to the MiG-21 in layout, and only slightly larger. Accordingly, though other types were studied, the *Sapfir* family was from the outset the front runner for a MiG-21 interceptor.

Thus, in late 1957, just as the Gorkii factory was engaged in the make-ready stage of the series production line of the first MiG-21F fighters, the MiG OKB began full-scale development of the Ye-7, a MiG-21 fitted with another radar of the *Sapfir* family. Ye-7 studies on paper had begun more than a year earlier, but had generally run into severe problems caused by the centre of gravity (cg) being too far forward. By 1957 the weight estimates of installed radars included some that were light enough to look promising. The MiG OKB had already gathered a considerable amount of experience from tunnel testing, and from numerous earlier and parallel prototypes, so there was not expected to be any difficulty in the aerodynamic or structural redesign of the nose. There remained a major cg problem, especially as there was

A trio of Czech Republic MiG-21s. Nearest to the camera are a pair of 'PFMs – the nearest one wearing a special paint scheme; with a MiG-21US two-seater in the background.
Russian Aviation Research Trust

strong pressure to increase internal fuel capacity, and it was easier to add capacity at the front (as was then being done in the Ye-66A) rather than at the tail. On the other hand, removing the remaining gun helped, and a solution began to look possible.

In 1958-59 the MiG OKB's Factory No.155 built three Ye-7 prototypes. These were based on the Ye-6T, but had airframes restressed to the higher load factor of 7.8. Apart from the completely new nose, the only significant modification to the basic aircraft was to increase the size of the main landing wheels, the KT-50/2 having tyres increased in diameter from 660 to 800mm (31½in), width remaining 200mm. These larger tyres were inflated to a maximum of only 0.785MPa (115lb/in²), the objective being to match heavier future versions of MiG-21 to weakly paved runways and pavements. They required significantly larger blisters above the wing and in the wheel bay door. The nose gear was unaltered.

The fuselage was modified by finally eliminating the right hand gun and the two gun fairings. Never to return, their absence simplified

the design of the forward airbrakes, which were also enlarged to 0.422m² (4.54ft²) each. Frames Nos.25 and 28 were modified for the attachment of two SU-1500 assisted take-off rockets, as tested on the two Ye-6V prototypes. Not least, the first concession was made to electronic complexity by the addition (not at first fitted to Ye-7/1) of an autopilot, though the KAP-1 selected was a single-axis system with authority in the roll axis only.

A basic objective with the Ye-7 prototypes was to produce a fighter capable of at least some degree of autonomous operation, and able to seek out and destroy hostile aircraft at night or in adverse weather. This required more than just a short-range radar, and, as was being done with several other aircraft at this time, a *kompleks* (an integrated electronic system) was assembled for the future MiG-21 interceptor. At the outset this comprised the experimental TsD-30T radar, a TACAN-type navigation aid called KSI, an improved *Lazur* (Azure) beam and beacon receiver linked with the *Vozdukh*-1 (Air-1) air defence ground network, a waveform receiver, the SOD-57M decimetric responder

At Zhukovskii near sunset, 'Red 71', the Ye-7/1, was the first of the interceptors. Unusually, its fin cap antenna was of black glass fibre. Note K-13 missiles, PVD boom hinged under the nose, and small wing tip pods.

The second interceptor, 'Red 72', had a coloured nose cone, painted inlet lip, silver fin cap antenna and smaller red star on the fin.

Head-on view of Ye-7/2, with what looks like Ostapenko in the cockpit. The inlet diameter of 870mm (2ft 10¼in) was almost the same as that of the fuselage. All Yefim Gordon archive

and the unchanged *Khrom* IFF, *Sirena*-2 RWR, SRO-2 transponder, MRP-56P marker receiver and RSIU-5V radio.

For obvious reasons the future interceptor, to be designated MiG-21P (from *Perekhvatchik*, interceptor) was still going to be limited in what it could do. The basic problem of short range and endurance could not be overcome in so small an aircraft, though over the years more and more fuel was to be added. The same

Though seen before, this picture is interesting because it shows what may be a non-flying airframe used for radar training. Labelled *Trenazher* (Simulator), it has no PVD boom nor any radio or IFF antennas.
Bill Gunston archive

A Ye-7 prototype serving as a cutaway instructional airframe at the Moscow Aviation Institute. The K-15 missile under its wing was actually carried by the huge Lavochkin La-250 'Anaconda' seen in the background.

A cutaway Tumanskii R-11F2S-300, surrounded by instructional displays. The large disc amidships, on a perforated ring, is one of the bleed connections.

'Red/white 04' was one of the small batch of MiG-21PFS. It has the extension strips at top and bottom of the nozzle.
All three Yefim Gordon archive

dimensional factor made it impossible to install1 a really large high power radar, so the MiG-21P was still going to need guidance from the ground to a point quite near – a maximum of something like 10km (6 miles) – and preferably astern of its target. This meant that it could not operate except over the more threatened parts of the Soviet Union where *Vozdukh* coverage was available. Finally, though in time of actual armed conflict this would have been a secondary factor, the MiG-21P could not land in blind conditions.

Despite these limitations, the fitting of the new *kompleks* would obviously multiply the effectiveness of what by 1960 was accepted – certainly in the Soviet Union – as probably the best close air combat fighter in the world. This was a peculiar time, when the minds of many in authority were polarised around guided missiles. In Britain, as noted earlier, this reached such a lunatic level that it was concluded that no more manned fighters would ever be needed. In the USA and some other countries it was believed that AAMs made it unnecessary to fit fighters with guns.

To some degree the revolution in thinking about fighter armament was caused not so much by the emergence of effective and reliable AAMs as by the increasing flight performance of fighter aircraft. There appeared to be a lot of sense in the argument that, if fighters could fly at Mach 2, there could be no such thing as close combat, because the minimum radius of turn of such a fast aircraft would be several kilometres. It was reasoned that the only possible way to kill such fast opponents would be to fire a missile from a distance. Nowhere was this belief more strongly adhered to than in the Soviet Union. None of the heavy radar-equipped interceptors then in production for the IA-PVO – the Yak-28P, Su-9 and Su-11, and the forthcoming Tu-128, Su-15 and MiG-25P – carried any guns, though some were modified later to carry guns as external stores.

Thus, there were those who wondered if perhaps the MiG-21, born out of close dogfights over Korea, might not have been an outdated concept. Adding radar and AAMs seemed the only way to go. On the other hand, the MiG OKB was delighted to have built up an export business, first with the MiG-15 and its trainer version, later with the MiG-17 and MiG-19. Now, with the MiG-21 having such good prospects that the *Znamya Truda* plant had been assigned solely in order to meet export orders. The MiG-21P promised to be almost what several important foreign customers – especially India – had been asking for.

The main problem was that some of these customers were not entirely happy at the prospect of a fighter without guns. Whereas in the USSR there was almost no way ordinary front-line pilots could feed back their opinions and problems to Moscow, foreign customers could tell the MiG OKB directly. India, and later others, wanted a gun. Eventually conflicts in South East Asia and the Middle East were to prove them right.

The key element in the MiG-21P was the radar. Though the Volkov bureau was the biggest engaged in developing fighter radars, it was the Nyenartovich KB that was responsible for the TsD-30, one of the first members of the *Sapfir* family and specially tailored to the MiG-21P. The production version for the MiG-21 was to be designated RP-21. Features included a

single parabolic antenna of about 550mm (22in) diameter, mechanically scanned in a raster (or zig-zag) form through ±30° in azimuth (30° left to 30° right) whilst searching through a vertical angular distance which could be as great as ±60° but normally extended from 15° above the aircraft's longitudinal axis to 15° below.

Both the TsD-30 and the series RP-21 were designed to operate in four modes, search, acquisition (locked on), pursuit tracking and fire control (in Russian, called 'taking aim' mode). In the search mode this radar operated at a pulse repetition frequency (PRF) of 825-950Hz, with a brochure ability to detect a 16m² (172ft²) target at a distance of 20 km (12½ miles). In the pursuit mode, tail on to a typical jet target, the effective range was expected to be 10km (6.2 miles). Once locked on, the RP-21

switched to a PRF of 1,750-1,850Hz. Bright phosphors were not then available, so to use the radar in daylight the pilot had to bend his head to a circular visor, shutting out most of the light. In the 1960s learning about radar was a completely new task for about 27,000 pilots and back-seaters, and a much greater number of ground engineers, in VVS Frontal Aviation, the IA-PVO and *Aviatsiya Voenno-Morskovo Flota* (A-VMF (Naval Aviation).

Accommodating the radar demanded a very large increase in the size of the inlet centre-body. As there was no change in the engine, the maximum airflow remained 65kg (143lb) per second. To pass this around the larger centre-body required an increase in the diameter of the inlet from 690 to 870mm (34¼in). It also demanded an increase in fuselage length, the distance from the inlet lip to the tail nozzle rising from 12,177mm to 12,290mm (40ft 3⅞in).

The centre-body fixed portion was constructed mainly from the usual D16-T, but based upon rings of magnesium alloy. These carried the needle roller bearings for the sliding beams that carried the translating cone. They were attached to a D16-T ring forming the base for the cone itself, made of glass-fibre re-inforced plastics with high transparency to the chosen wavelengths. The cone was now so important that its external profile was made of Oswatitsch type, the main cone leading at its rear end to narrow rings with progressively greater angle to give efficient multi-shock deceleration of the airflow at the highest flight Mach numbers. It was installed with its axis pointing 3° down relative to the longitudinal axis of the fuselage. This was calculated to be the optimum compromise for maximum pressure recovery at all AoA.

As before, the cone was translated hydraulically according to flight Mach number, but because of its much greater size the control system was replaced by the more powerful UVD-2M. Another change was the need to cool the radar. This was done by providing a bleed ring surrounding the base of the cone through which boundary-layer air could be sucked by aft-facing ejectors above and below the nose. Normally this airflow cooled the radar, but at Mach numbers over 1.35 it could be shut off by pneumatically-actuated valves, the ram air at such speeds becoming too hot to be useful. No MiG-21 was expected to hold supersonic speeds for long, due to limited fuel capacity.

The Ye-7/1, call-sign 'Red 71', was first flown by Ostapenko on 10th August 1958. It had an inert mass in the inlet centre-body to simulate the radar. Most of the other modifications were incorporated, though like the Ye-7/2 the vertical tail was the original small chord type. Almost all the test flights with Ye-7/1 were with the objective of proving the new inlet. A minor problem was that the increased length of inlet ahead of the PVD forward mount greatly reduced the possible angular movement of the boom when disconnected at the rear mount on the ground, so that damage from vehicles and other hazards had to be considered. It was decided in

ngine stalls and flame-outs caused by tran-
ent excursions in yaw.

To expand the possible range of weapon fits,
e radar was replaced by the RP-21M. This
ad a guidance function for compatible radar
ommand-guided missiles, notably the RS-
US (K-51) AAM, which was rapidly approach-
g obsolescence but was available in large
umbers for training purposes, and the Kh-23
Kompleks 66) for precision attack of surface
rgets. This dramatically improved the air-
raft's versatility, but many pilots considered an
ven greater advance was to offer the option of
gun, an excellent new design by V P Gryasev
nd A G Shipunov, able to fire 23mm ammuni-
on with high velocity from twin barrels at the
yclic rate of 3,600 rounds/min. This gun, the
elf-powered and electrically fired GSh-23, was
ackaged together with its cooling, control sys-
m and a 200 round magazine into a quickly
emovable pack with the designation GP-9.
his could be attached scabbed on to the
nderside of the mid-fuselage in an installation
sted on Ye-7s and MiG-21PFs. To increase
un aiming accuracy an improved sight was fit-
d, the ASP-PF-21, also called simply PKI.

There were numerous other modifications.
hese included the introduction of *Khrom-Nikel*
RO-2M IFF and *Sirena*-3M radar warning, the
ain passive receivers of which were mounted
n the rear ends of the GIK magnetometer blis-
rs on each side of the fin. For short take-offs it
as possible to attach an SPRD-99 rocket on
ach side of the fuselage, secured to the
nchorages previously used for the more pow-
ful SU-1500. The thrust of each rocket was
5t (5,511lb) for up to 17 seconds. These rock-
s were used in VVS service.

A simplified version of the MiG-21PFM (not
e PF, as often reported) was prepared for
cence-construction by Hindustan Aeronautics
d (HAL), in India. Whereas the Indian Air
orce had used the MiG-21F-13, all these had
een imported from the Soviet Union. Organis-
g production of the fighter in India, under an
greement signed in 1962, was a colossal task
volving a new group of factories at Koraput
ngines), Hyderabad (avionics and instru-
ents) and Nasik (airframe, final assembly and
ght test).

G-21PF-V interceptors during the Vietnam
ar. Yefim Gordon archive

ke-off by a Type 94 MiG-21PFM in Vietnam.
fim Gordon archive

ssibly Colonel Toom's aircraft, this Type 94
ears 12 stars (but an earlier aircraft, PF-V
.4326, bore 13).
ussian Aviation Research Trust

ke-off by a MiG-21PFM Type 94, with KM-1
at and side-hinged canopy with fixed
indscreen. Yefim Gordon archive

The initial version produced by HAL (desig
nated MiG-21FL, Type 77) featured the R-11F
300 engine, simpler R-2L radar and greater fue
capacity of 2,900 litres (637.9 gal). Initial ai
craft, followed by CKD kits for Indian assembl
were made in Moscow in 1965-68. Indian pro
duction of this version took place in 1966-73.

Production of the MiG-21PFM for the VV
began at Gorkii in late 1964. At the 15th aircra
a new design of seat became available. Thi
outstanding seat, the KM-1, still could not b
used at below 130km/h (81mph), but it coul
be fired at up to 1,200km/h (745mph) indicate
airspeed, and at any height down to groun
level. It proved to be very reliable, and did n
need the canopy to protect the pilot, which ha
never been fully satisfactory. The canopy wa
redesigned with a strong fixed windscreen an
a separate main canopy hinged open sideway
to the right. The modified cockpit encroache
slightly on fuselage tank No.1, reducing inte
nal fuel capacity to 2,650 litres (583 gal). Ai
craft with the new seat and canopy were d Typ
94s. Another modification introduced durin
production was the KT-102 nosewheel, with n
change in tyre size but with the brake change
to a more powerful disc type.

The MiG-21PFM was to have been the ne
standard aircraft, but in fact only a year later
was replaced on the production line by st
newer versions. Corresponding export mode
were produced by the *Znamya Truda* facto
from 1966-68. At an airshow at Mosco
Domodyedovo in 1967 a MiG-21PFM (call-sig
'78') demonstrated take-offs without rocket
and with partial reheat (the ground run bein
850-1,350m or 2,788-4,429ft), with SPRD-9
rockets and full reheat (360-430m or 1,181
1,410ft), and landings with wheel brakes onl
(ground run 1,100-1,250m or 3,608-4,101ft
then brakes and parabrake (850-950m c
2,788-3,116ft) and finally brakes and parabrak
after an SPS approach (420-500m or 1,377
1,640ft). (MiG-21Ye and M-21 conversions ar
covered in Chapter 13.)

Top: **From 1960 pilots of the IA-PVO, unlike
those of Frontal Aviation, wore partial-pressure
suits and sealed helmets.**
Russian Aviation Research Trust

Second down: **Unusual MiG-21PFM, this time in
dark blue/grey camouflage for evaluation by the
A-VMF at Saki, Crimea. It has call-sign 'Red 42',
ahead of the navy flag.** G F Petrov archive

Above, left: **Lubianyi and (left) A Stashkov pose
with a MiG-21PFM in September 1969. This is a
good close-up of the inlet, with PVD boom
centrally above.** Bill Gunston archive

Above, right: **Take-off by a MiG-21PFM with a
single rocket on the centre-line.**
Yefim Gordon archive

Below: **'Red 503' is not a VVS aircraft but an ex-
Hungarian Air Force 'PF imported by the UK
aviation film industry specialist Aces High in
the spring of 1989 and typical of the many dis-
posals to 'warbird' operators and museums
from that time onwards.** Ken Ellis collection

New Generation Fighters

...y 1960, before any MiG-21s were in opera-...onal service, the MiG OKB could see a series ...f possible improvements and modifications, ...nough nobody could have predicted just how ...umerous and long-lasting these would be! ...he overall aerodynamics and flight control ...ere judged to be outstanding, and as early as ...957 the more basic problems posed by fitting ...earch radar were regarded as essentially ...olved. Almost all the other pressures for ...hange were concerned with engine thrust, ...eapons and, especially, internal fuel capacity. ...ut it so happened that the first member of ...hat might be called the third-generation fami-...was to fit the aircraft for a totally different role. ...In the late 1950s the FA had plenty of tactical ...conaissance aircraft. Almost all were of two

types. The Ilyushin Il-28R 'Beagle' had useful range but was subsonic and relatively easy to shoot down. The Yakovlev Yak-27R 'Mangrove' was again large, though for short periods at medium and high altitudes it could exceed Mach 1, but it was expensive and only 180 were built. In addition there were a handful of MiG-19R single-seaters, with shorter range and unable to operate at night or in bad weather. What was wanted was a survivable platform that combined supersonic speed with night and all weather capability.

From 1955 the OKB of P V Tsybin had been developing the RSR, a reconnaissance aircraft able to fly at great heights at nearly Mach 3 (a predecessor of the Lockheed SR-71 Black-bird). This was more strategic in nature, and likely to be very costly, and in 1959-61 its funds were transferred by the Kremlin to strategic missiles, until it eventually ground to a halt just before first flight. Frontal Aviation could never have operated anything like the Tsybin RSR. It wanted tough serviceable machines able to rough it with other front-line aviation regiments.

Mikoyan was convinced that the need could

be met by a new version of the MiG-21, to be designated MiG-21R (*Razvedchik*, reconnais-sance). Studies for such an aircraft began in the late 1950s, and from the outset a key factor was that there should be minimal change to the air-frame. The reconnaissance sensors were to be carried in a pod (a streamlined container) hung under the centre-line. This would preclude the use of a centre-line drop tank, and to obtain adequate range the wings would be plumbed to enable four drop tanks to be carried on four underwing pylons, the outer pylons being new additions.

Such an arrangement had much to com-mend it. With five external stores, aerodynamic drag would obviously increase significantly, but not enough to cause serious loss of perfor-mance. Speed at very low level would still be about Mach 0.95, while at high altitude it might reach about Mach 1.6, both figures being fully acceptable and determined mainly by the pay-load limits rather than by lack of engine thrust. Packaging the sensors into a pod would enable various types of pod to be produced for differ-ent types of mission, a particular pattern being

Top left: **The first reconnaissance MiG-21 was Ye-7/8, the eighth Ye-7 prototype. It combined the old MiG-21PFS airframe with the new parabrake installation, a unique round-topped fin cap antenna and five pylons which here are loaded with a Type-R pod, two tanks and two R-3S missiles.**

Top right: **MiG-21R head-on, showing the PVD boom moved to the right side; the wing tip electronic warfare antenna containers can also be seen clearly. Inboard pylons are fitted but empty.**

Above: **MiG-21R 'Red 22', seen from below carrying two tanks and a D-type pod. The wing tip antenna pods stand out clearly.**

Left: **A series MiG-21R, Type 94R, with KM-1 seat and new canopy, spine, fin and cap antenna, wing tip receiver antenna pods and AoA sensor on the left side of the nose. It is carrying a Type-D pod, and (as was common) has the inboard pylons removed.**

All Yefim Gordon archive

quickly clipped on the aircraft according to the needs of the moment. Equipping the wing with four pylons would give the local commander even more flexibility in choosing where necessary to fit two tanks and two missiles.

As noted in the previous chapter, the first flight tests of this scheme were carried out with the Ye-7/8 prototype. Apart from the four-pylon wing, this differed from other early MiG-21PF aircraft in several respects. Most importantly, though it retained the one-piece canopy and intermediate-chord (4.08m^2 – 43.9ft^2) fin, it had the R-11F2S-300 engine and SPS blown flaps. The fin had a redesigned top made of fibre-reinforced plastics forming a large flush antenna. This curved over at the top to carry a modified streamlined fairing for the other fin top antennas and fuel vent. This design of fin had previously flown on the Ye-8, see Chapter 10.

In sharp contrast to previous MiG-21s, the Ye-7/8 had four wing stations all plumbed for drop tanks, and it was tested with four of the 490 litre (107.8 gal) size. The inboard stations were also wired for AAMs, as an alternative load, and the pylon could have an APU-13 or

APU-13MT interface shoe for, respectively, an R-3R or R-3S self-defence missile. On the other hand, the centre-line pylon had a fuel connection, but no weapon capability. Instead it had a multi-pin socket and attachments for any of four families of sensor pod. Of course, all four containers were roughly the same size, having a pointed nose, irregular shape in side elevation, oval cross section with a flat underside, a long pylon interface on top, and a shallow dorsal fin at the tail. It was not intended that any pod should be jettisoned in flight.

The first patterns to be tested, and the most numerous in subsequent Frontal Aviation service, were the D (day), N (night) and R (radio). The D family of pods were for daylight optical photography. Each normally accommodated seven cameras, typically six A-39 or AFA-39 and one AShTShAFA-SM for strip coverage which could if necessary be extended to either horizon. Under the pod's nose was an oblique flat window for a forward-looking camera, causing a sharp kink in the outline. The other six cameras were arranged in pairs in three successive heated bays, looking through windows

in the flat bottom. Many different kinds of film were available, some sensitive to infra-red, heat radiation (IR). In addition most D pods carried SPO-3R passive radar receiver antennas covering 360° in azimuth, as well as radar monitoring and countermeasures, which could include an ASO-2I chaff/flare dispenser. Later D-type pods housed electro-optical (TV) sensors and/or IR linescan. Typical D-series pods weighed 285kg (628lb).

As their 'radio' designation prefix suggested, the R-series pods were concerned primarily with electronic surveillance. In all cases a single A-39 camera was carried in the forward oblique position, but the window was further back than in the D-series and set at a shallower angle, giving the pod a smoother outline. Major sensors were sideways-looking airborne radars (SLARs) of the *Lyra* family, installed at mid length with antennas scanning on either or on both sides. Comprehensive radio and radar

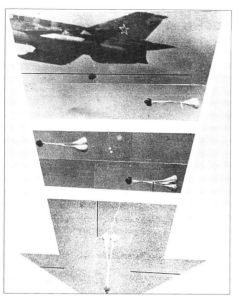

Above: **Final assembly of Type 75 MiG-21*bis* fighters at the Nasik plant of Hindustan Aeronautics. With this aircraft HAL strove to become self-sufficient.** Yefim Gordon archive

Below: **MiG-21*bis* 'Blue 09' in special markings and carrying the badge of the MiG OKB in the nose, on display amid weaponry, September 1993.** Viktor Drusklyakov

Chapter Nine

'Sparka' – The Trainers

A contrived photograph, but nevertheless showing off the main attributes of MiG-21U *Sparka* **'Green 66'.** Yefim Gordon archive

Above: **Official NII side view of the Ye-6U/1, with a 490 litre tank and APU-13 rails loaded with R-3S missiles. The Red Star was smaller than standard.**

Left: **A big fin MiG-21US in service at a VVS pilot school. It has three empty pylons, and one of the blown-flap actuator fairings has caught the sunlight.**

Below left: **'Red 64' was the Ye-6U/4, the fourth Type 66 two-seat MiG-21. It is seen in use as an LII platform for photo and TV work, in this case flying as chase aircraft to an Su-9U used for ejection seat trials.**

Bottom: **This MiG-21US, Type 68, has extra equipment (such as the AoA sensor and instructor periscope) making it look like a MiG-21UM. It has no UHF blade antenna.**
All Yefim Gordon archive

Photographs on the opposite page:

MiG-21US serving as a testbed for equipment trials. It is a single-seater, the rear cockpit carrying the special equipment which also includes a puzzling blister and fairing on the right side of the fuselage. Trials are recorded by a camera on the fin. The wing pylon is of a deep MiG-23 type. Yefim Gordon archive

Snow-encrusted VVS MiG-21US in three-tone camouflage. Note the call-sign number ('White 204' repeated on the fin and 'keel'. Yefim Gordon

Prior to the 1960s the standard jet trainer in all advanced pilot schools throughout the Soviet Union was the MiG-15UTI 'Midget'. Though it might have seemed an awesome challenge to a pupil who had never flown a jet – and most VVS pupils had previously graduated on the Czech Aero L-29 Delfin (NATO reporting name 'Maya') or the Aero L-39 Albatros – the MiG-15UTI was a simple, reliable and low cost stepping stone to operational types. It was, of course, sub-sonic.

In contrast, there were dual trainer versions of all the Sukhoi aircraft in front-line service. When the decision was taken to put the MiG-21, a Mach 2 delta, into production there could no longer be any argument. In 1958 Mikoyan asked his team to consider a dual control trainer version, and various studies ensued. The optimum arrangement, *Izdelye* 66, was launched in November 1959, and the Ye-6U/1 prototype was flown by Pyotr M Ostapenko on 17th October 1960.

As far as possible the trainer was identical with the series MiG-21F, though it was designed to the reduced load factor of 7.0. The fuselage length from inlet to nozzle remained 12.177mm, and the engine was still the R-11F-300. Nevertheless, the fuselage had to be redesigned between Frames Nos.6 and 22 to accommodate the pupil in the front cockpit (in the original position), the instructor in an added rear cockpit and revised fuel tankage.

No attempt was made to raise the rear instructor cockpit significantly to improve his forward view. Both cockpits were very similar, but it was no longer possible to use the canopy as a windbreak, so the SK seats were standard. In front of the pupil was a fixed windshield with a near oval flat front screen, though this differed slightly from that adopted later on single-seat MiG-21s. Above each cockpit was a separate long canopy hinged to the right. Unlike the Ye-6U/1 prototype, production trainer canopies could be locked open by a stay. A flat transparent windbreak between the cockpits carried the pressure seals for the rear edge of the pupil's canopy and the front of the instructor's, and protected the instructor in the event of loss of the rear canopy, but it was not strong enough to serve as a crash arch.

The inlet to the engine duct was unchanged from that of the MiG-21F, but the PVD boom was moved to the central position above it, and no longer pivoted. For training pupils in firing a gun the SRD-5 ranging radar and ASP-5ND sight were installed, but the devastating NR-30 cannon was a case of overkill. This gun and its magazine were removed, and replaced when necessary by a pod carried on the centreline pylon housing a single A-12.7 heavy machine gun and its ammunition. The twin forward airbrakes were replaced by a single large brake on the centre-line. As the trainers were to be lighter, deceleration with air brake was actually enhanced. The main wheels were of the larger 700mm type introduced on the Ye-7/MiG-21P, requiring large blisters in the fuselage and doors. Avionics were simple, and generally the same as those of the MiG-21F-13, the downward *Khrom* IFF antenna being immediately behind the nose gear bay. The autopilot was the KAP-2, with authority in roll only. The parabrake was in the underside of the fuselage.

Another result which at first sight seems remarkable is that internal fuel capacity, far from being greatly reduced, was actually increased. A large metal fuel tank was inserted between fuselage Frames Nos.14-22, extending upwards to occupy the capacious but sharply tapered fairing behind the instructor's canopy, augmenting the five flexible cells between Frames Nos.14-28. This was partly made possible by deleting the cannon and fitting a single airbrake. Thus, internal fuel rose to 2,350 litres (517 gal), or 1,950kg. In the production aircraft it was to rise further. Like all trainers, the wing was fitted to carry K-13 missiles, rocket pods, bombs or drop tanks on a single pylon on each side.

The Ye-6U/1, call-sign 'Red 61', was soon joined by Ye-6U/2, with a telemetry antenna under the forward fuselage. Development posed few problems, and OKB testing lasted little over nine months. A large order was placed for the series aircraft, designated MiG-21U, with OKB product number Type 66. (*Uchyebnii* – trainer. ASCC reporting name 'Mongol'.) Fresh production capacity had to be found, and the choice fell on Factory No.31 at Tbilisi, capital of Georgia. Series manufacture began here in 1962, and output of this initial version terminated with No.180 in 1966. All series aircraft had the PVD boom moved to the right above the nose. To fulfil export orders, the *Znamya Truda* factory built the MiG-21U in parallel with fighter versions during 1964-68.

From the outset the trainer was dubbed *Sparka* (Twin). Despite its low power the MiG-21U had quite a good performance, with speed and handling almost indistinguishable from the corresponding single-seater. In 1965 one of the first was retrofitted with an uprated engine and used to set women's records. On 22nd May 1965 Natalya Prokhanova set a dynamic (zoom trajectory) height record at 24,336m (79,843ft). On 23rd June Lydia Zaitseva held a sustained altitude of 19,020m (62,402ft). The latter compares with the brochure service ceiling of 18.3km (60,039ft). The aircraft was reported to the FAI as the Ye-33, though this was never a designation assigned by the MiG bureau (apparently, some official chose to halve Ye-66!).

During production of the MiG-21U the nose-wheel was changed to the disc-braked KT-102. Quite early in Tbilisi production, and later at the Moscow factory, the trainers were fitted with the final (5.2m² – 55.9²) broad vertical tail, with the parabrake (often of the improved cruciform type) relocated in the tube below the rudder.

In 1966 the Tbilisi factory switched to making the upgraded MiG-21US, Type 68. As its designation implied, this was fitted with the R-11F2S-300 engine and SPS blown flaps. The aircraft did not really need blown flaps, but it was highly desirable to train pilots in SPS operation, even including making landings at maximum flap angle with full blowing. As no radar was fitted, the inlet and sliding cone remained essentially unchanged, inlet diameter staying at 690mm.

Among several other changes in the MiG-21US were a slight increase in internal fuel capacity to 2,450 litres (539 gal) or 2,030kg, the option of fitting four pylons, and the installation of a new crew-escape system. In the front cockpit the pupil had a KM-1U seat, while the instructor had a KM-1I, both being versions of the SK-3. A lever on the right hand coaming in each cockpit could initiate the ejection sequence and blow off both canopies, this action automatically arming the seats. The pupil, however, could not eject the instructor. Like other KM-1 versions, these seats could be used at all altitudes, but not below a speed of 130km/h (80mph).

In 1974, long after the later MiG-21UM was available, the Ye-6US development aircraft, fitted with an R-11F2S-300 engine uprated to 7t (15,432lb) thrust, was used for women's time-to-height records. On 6th June Svetlana Savitskaya achieved times to 3, 6, 9, and 12km (9,843, 19,685, 29,528 and 39,370ft) of 59.1

seconds, 1 min 20.4 sec, 1 min 46.7 sec and 2 min 35.1 sec. On 15th November she bettered these figures to, respectively, 41.2 sec, 1 min 0.1 sec, 1 min 21 sec and 1 min 59.3 sec. The reason for the better figures is that on the second occasion the aircraft was fitted with 'two TTRD of 2,300kg', these being SPRD-99 assisted take-off rockets, which of course were jettisoned on burnout.

Production of the MiG-21US took place only at Tbilisi, for both home and export customers, the total built being 347. In the course of production a modification was made which many instructors had requested from 1962. Their view ahead was even worse than that from the cluttered front cockpit of single-seaters, making it difficult for them to take charge on take-off or, especially, on landing. The answer was a large and simple periscope, the operation of which was linked with the landing gear. When gear was selected down, the upper mirror was pulled open above the canopy and the lower

mirror hinged down inside from the front, both mirrors being linked by a system of rods and hinged to a new metal top to the canopy.

The final trainer version, the MiG-21UM, Type 69, was again manufactured only at Tbilisi, which in 1971-75 produced 1,133. This naturally incorporated all the previous upgrades, and added numerous additional or improved items of equipment, almost all of them being concerned with the cockpit or avionics. The externally obvious additions were the DUA-3A AoA sensor on the left side of the nose and the blade antenna for R-832 VHF on the spine in front of the fin. The cockpit instrumentation was completely modernised, and other upgrades included fitting the AP-155 three-axis autopilot and an ASP-PFD sight for the pupil. To facilitate servicing, most avionics were mounted on quickly removable racking.

Altogether the *Sparka* family proved both a commercial and operational success. Every

one of the 40-odd air forces which used the MiG-21 also used the trainer. As well as its basic duty of conversion to type, it proved excellent at teaching aerobatics at all speeds up to well beyond Mach 1, blind flying at all speeds, and also simple air-to-air and air-to-ground weapon delivery. A number have also been used as testbeds, one Czech example being used to develop a Czech ejection seat, fired from the rear cockpit.

Chapter Ten

Experimentals

In addition to the prototypes already described, which could be described as experimental but whose research and test flying was concerned with developing the series versions, the MiG-21 was also used as the basis for five aircraft in three families whose purpose was experimental in the fullest sense. All were grossly modified, so that they bore only a superficial resemblance to the original MiG-21.

Before describing these aircraft, it is appropriate to report on various less fundamental

Analog, or Imitator, the MiG-21I experimental was designed to pave the way for the so-called 'Concordski', the Tupolev Tu-144 supersonic airliner. The survivor of two Is is displayed at Monino. Yefim Gordon archive.

research programmes flown by otherwise standard MiG-21s. One of these was the testing of skis. Because winter in many parts of the Soviet Union is so severe and prolonged, it had always been important for as many landplanes as possible to be cleared to operate from ice and compacted snow on skis. With supersonic jets this has been much more difficult to achieve, partly because of the higher take-off and landing speeds, and the need for directional stability during long ground runs, but chiefly because in most cases it has proved impossible to make the skis fully retractable. Despite this, it was VVS policy to try to qualify *all* tactical aircraft to operate from the shortest possible unpaved airstrips even when contaminated by snow. Extensive ski testing took place in 1960 using the Ye-5/2 prototype. Sadly, no photographs have yet been found, and what is especially strange is that the tests took place from May to July!

The skis, of two types, were fitted to the main legs only, and no attempt was made to make them retractable. One design was almost rectangular, with an upturned front. The other was circular, with an upturned rim all round, because this pattern was free to rotate. The test programme was entrusted to OKB pilot Igor M Kravtsov, and the skis were changed after each flight. The greatest difficulty was encountered in taxying, when it proved almost impossible to maintain control of either pointing attitude or direction of travel. Eventually it was decided that the best answer for contaminated runways was the KL, wheel/ski arrangement, as used on the Su-7BKL. This used a steel ski hardly larger than the wheel, mounted on its own shock struts at a steep nose-up angle. KL landing gear can retract inside the normal wheel bay.

In 1965 Kravtsov was killed in the MiG Ye-152A, a twin-engined delta unrelated to the MiG-21. Further ski testing was carried out in

Dassault Mirages and McDonnell Douglas F-4 Phantoms – which unquestionably would have been more fault-prone, and far more difficult and costly to maintain.

At the same time, one cannot stop the clock, especially in so fast-moving a field of technology as supersonic fighters. After considering various alternatives, the Chinese Ministry of Aero-Space Industry decided in the late 1970s on a two-pronged approach to keep the local products competitive. One was to emulate the MiG OKB in developing a fighter resembling the MiG-21MF/Type 96F. Work on this aircraft, called J-7 III, began in 1981. The other, which was generally preferred, was to change the basic aircraft as little as possible, but to upgrade it in detail and, most importantly, fit a totally new suite of avionics. Some of the new avionics items were imported as early as May 1979, but actual development of the upgraded aircraft, called F-7M, began in parallel with the J-7 III in 1981. In 1986 this version was given the name Airguard.

Dealing with the basic aircraft first, the Airguard still retains the original 690mm nose inlet, precluding installation of a search radar, as well as the 4.08m² (43.9ft²) fin as fitted to the later MiG-21F-13, and almost the same fuel system, with capacity fractionally reduced from 2,470 to 2,385 litres (524.5 gal). Surprisingly, the main tyres are even smaller than those of the original Soviet aircraft, with a diameter of only 600mm (23.62in), and the resulting inflation pressure of 1.15 MPa (166.8 lb/in²) prohibits operations from anything but paved runways. On the other hand, many modifications have been made. The wing is equipped for four pylons. The seat is the CAC zero-height pattern, based on the Soviet SK, usable at all speeds from 130-850 km/h (80-528mph) indicated. The air data boom has been moved to the right side above the nose, and is no longer pivoted. The tailplane anti-flutter masses are shorter and less-pointed.

The engine is the WP-7B(BM), with ratings unchanged but incorporating important improvements. The most welcome was elimination of the need for a separate starting fuel tank and supply system using petrol (gasoline). Total engine weight was reduced, and 40 afterburner firings are permitted in each 200 hour period.

Though still equipped solely with traditional electro-mechanical dial instruments, the cockpit of the Airguard is completely updated. At top centre is the head-up display and weapon-aiming computer (HUDWAC), which is the GEC-Marconi Type 956. The same company supplied the AD.3400 two-band UHF/VHF multi-function communications radio, with high security measures. Other new avionics items

included GMAv Type 226 Skyranger target-ranging radar, incorporating new electronic counter-countermeasures (ECCM), an angle-of-attack sensor on the left side of the nose, an air-data computer, WL-7 radio compass, XS-6A marker beacon receiver, Type 602 IFF transponder and Type 0101 HR-A/2 radar altimeter. Some of these were derived from Soviet designs. To match the improved avionics the electrical system required upgrading, four rotary inverters being replaced by three static examples. The Jianghuai YX-3 gaseous oxygen system is fitted.

The standard Airguard is fitted with two Type 30-1 guns, each with 60 rounds, in an installation almost identical to the original MiG-21F. The four wing pylons can accommodate PL-2, -2A, -2B, -5 or -7 or Magic AAMs, or either the 18 x 57mm or 7 x 90mm rocket launchers, or bombs up to the 500kg (1,102lb) type. The centre-line pylon can carry a 500 or 800 litre (110 or 176 gal) tank, and the outer wing pylons the 500 litre size.

After several years of development, the F-7M Airguard was publicly revealed in October 1984. Important orders were soon placed by Egypt, Iran, Bangladesh, Myanmar (formerly Burma) and Zimbabwe. The Pakistan Air Force (PAF) ordered a variant designated F-7P, which was briefly given the name Skybolt. This incorporates 24 modifications, the most important of which are Martin-Baker Mk.10L seats with zero-height, zero-airspeed capability, and the ability to fire four Sidewinder AAMs.

The latest PAF variant is the F-7MP, delivered in 1994-95. This has a new navigation and fire-control system, and an improved cockpit layout. From 1989 Rockwell Collins in the USA delivered 100 sets of new avionics, including the ARN-147 VOR/ILS receiver, ARN-149 ADF and ProLine II digital DME-42. FIAR in Italy supplied Grifo fire control radars, which fit inside the original small nose cone. All these items are fitted to the F-7MP, and will also be used to update the existing F-7P force.

Chronologically, the next major development was the launch in October 1982 of a Chinese version of the MiG-21US dual-control trainer. This was assigned to the Guizhou Aviation Industry Corporation (GAIC), which was already participating in the production of the

single-seaters. Naturally called the JJ-7, with FT-7 denoting the export version, this is basically a clone of the Soviet MiG-21US. It incorporates a periscope for the instructor, as on the MiG-21UM, as well as changes introduced by the F-7M Airguard, apart from absence of the AoA sensor. The instructor has control of a failure-simulation system.

The engine is the WP-7B(BM), fuel capacity is slightly greater than for the F-7M at 2440 litres (536.7 gal) but fractionally less than in the Soviet aircraft, and there is provision for three pylons for a maximum external load of 1,187kg (2,617lb), maximum external fuel being 558kg (1,230lb). A packaged Type 23-3 twin-barrel gun can be mounted on the centreline, aimed by an HK-03E optical sight. Other possible weapons include PL-2 or -2B missiles, HF-5A (18 x 57mm) rocket launchers, or bombs of 100 or 250kg.

The PAF trainer is the FT-7P. This has no instructor periscope, but has two pylons on each wing, an improved fire-control system incorporating the HUDWAC, and other cockpit improvements including the air-data computer. Increased fuel capacity "gives 25 per cent greater range".

After four years of development, the prototype J-7 III made its first flight on 26 April 1984. As already noted, this is almost a clone of the MiG-21MF, Mikoyan Type 96F. However, most of the equipment is Chinese and often by no means a direct copy of a Soviet original. For example, the engine is the WP-13, which, though it has several features similar to the Gavrilov R-13-300, was developed in China jointly by Chengdu Engine Co and LMC, and is in production by the latter. Afterburning rating is the same as for the Soviet counterpart at 6.6t (14,550lb), but maximum dry thrust is slightly greater at 4.1t (9,039lb).

Bleed air from the WP-13 supplies the blown flaps. Another major update is to enlarge the air inlet to accommodate a J-band radar designated JL-7. The broad 5.2m^2 (56ft^2) fin is fitted, and other changes include an HTY-4 'low-speed zero-height' seat, a canopy hinged open to the right and incorporating a rear view periscope, increased spine fuel and a Beijing Aeronautical Instruments KJ-11 two-channel (pitch and roll) autopilot.

The prototype F-7M Airguard. Russian Aviation Research Trust

79

Weapons can be carried on four wing pylons, the usual AAM being the PL-5B. Other loads can include HF-16B (12 x 57mm) or 7 x 90-mm rocket launchers, or two bombs of 500kg, four of 250kg or ten of 100kg (1,100, 550 and 220lb). A Type 23-3 gun pod can be carried on the centre-line, aimed by an HK-03D optical sight. Three 500 litre or one 800 litre (110 or 176 gal) external tanks can be carried. Avionics include the AoA sensor, an LJ-2 omni-directional RWR with its two aft-hemisphere passive antennas mounted on each side of the parabrake container (a feature not seen on any MiG-21), a GT-4 ECM jammer, Type 605A IFF (a copy of SRO-2), and an FJ-1 flight data recorder.

The J-7 III was developed jointly by CAC and GAIC, and by 1993 was in service with the PLAAF. The F-7 III is a further upgraded version, reported to be in service with both the PLAAF and Navy.

In 1987 CAC, the PAF and Grumman Corporation of the USA (now Northrop Grumman) carried out a study of a major J-7 redesign called Sabre 2, using an American engine and avionics. This led to a formal agreement on 21st October 1988 between the China National Aero-Technology Import and Export Corporation (CATIC) and Grumman for an aircraft called CAC Super-7. For political reasons, in 1989 the US Government terminated this collaboration (Chapter 13), but CATIC continued studies with the Pakistan Aeronautical Complex. Preliminary design and tunnel testing has been completed, and in mid-1995 the first flight was planned for 1996.

The modifications amount to a total redesign. The wing is not so much a delta as tapered on the leading edge, so that though span is increased to 8.98m (29ft 5½in), the area is increased only slightly to about 24.62m² (265 ft²). The new leading edge begins with a highly swept root extension and is fitted with slats over the main portion, and the tips carry launch rails for missiles (Sidewinder in the case of Pakistan). The capacious nose houses a powerful multi-mode radar, of a type not yet announced. Variable side inlets supply air to a completely different engine which several observers have predicted will be the Klimov RD-33, as used in the twin-engined MiG-29.

Other features include a redesigned fuel system, with optimised spine tankage and single-point pressure fuelling, a new nose gear with power steering, upgraded main gears, a modified ventral fin, arrester hook, an updated cockpit with an advanced HUD and new seat (this was expected to be the Martin-Baker Mk.10L, but will now be Russian, probably a K-36), comprehensive avionics with a revised cooling system, and with the two Type 30-1 guns replaced by an internal Type 23-3. Maximum take-off weight is predicted to be 11,295kg (24,900lb).

At the time of writing, in late 1995, the latest derivative of the basic J-7 is the J-7E. This incorporates wing features of the Super-7, the new outer panels (starting at the flap/aileron junction) having a leading-edge sweep of only 42°. A new feature is that these outer wings are also tapered slightly on the trailing edge, so that though span is increased to 8.32m (27ft 3½in), wing area is increased less than 2m² to 24.88m² (267.8ft²). This wing has four pylon stations, the outers plumbed for 480 litre (105 gal) tanks, and PL-8 AAMs can be carried. The engine is the WP-7F, with dry thrust considerably increased to 4.5t (9,921lb); rating with maximum afterburner is 6.5t (14,330lb), fractionally less than that of the WP-13. The J-7E is stressed for 8g up to Mach 0.8, and to 6.5g above this speed. Equipment includes digital avionics with a HUD and air data computer. No photographs of the J-7E had been released by mid-1995, though the prototype was said to have flown five years previously.

The Chinese industry threw down the gauntlet to the Mikoyan OKB. It made it clear that, throughout the foreseeable future, it would compete strongly with the A I Mikoyan complex and MAPO (see Chapter 13) in selling to Third World countries. The one thing the Chinese could not do was to produce an immediate rival to the all-new MiG-33 as a next-generation MiG-21 replacement. This clearly was a major factor in the unexpected decision of MiG-MAPO to 'get into bed with the Chinese' and work in partnership together!

As commented upon in the Introduction, this has major long term implications. The deal was struck in 1992, and Dr Aleksandr I Ageyev, MiG-MAPO's Director for Strategic Analysis, said in mid-1995 'We have discussed fitting the RD-33 and derived engines to Chinese fighters and fighter projects. We are assisting the Chinese to upgrade the MiG-21 into a fourth-generation aircraft with outstanding air combat and multi-role capability. We are also working with the growing Chinese industry on a new common design of Russo-Chinese fighter, the FC-1. We have done about 40% of the job, and expect to fly the prototype in about 2½ years'.

The baby J-12 was only distantly related to the MiG-21. Russian Aviation Research Trust

The display model of the FC-1, the remarkable fighter being developed jointly by CAC and MiG-MAPO. Paul A Jackson

A model of the Super-7, which since the departure of Grumman in 1989 has faded as an active project. Paul A Jackson

Chapter Twelve

In Combat

No fighter could serve so many air forces without becoming involved in a shooting war. It was the lot of the MiG-21 to engage many enemies, in three big conflicts and countless small ones. The big conflicts were the Indo-Pakistan wars, the *Yom Kippur* War between Israel and several Arab countries and the Vietnam War. The MiG-21 versions that fought in these conflicts were mainly of the PF/PFM type, plus a smaller number of MF/FL.

In a nutshell, the MiG-21 achieved significant success over India and Vietnam, but did less well in the Middle East, where the opposition was mainly the Mirage IIICJ. This is despite the fact that, in almost every respect, the MiG's flight performance and agility were superior to the French aircraft, though it was inferior in its radar, flight endurance and cockpit field of view. As in the case of the F-86 versus the MiG-15 in the Korean War, the poor showing of the MiG-21 against the IDF/AF was almost entirely due to a disparity between the combat training, experience and aggressive spirit of the Israeli pilots. Nevertheless, the results were distressing to the MiG OKB, even after analysis had shown the underlying cause.

The MiG-21 could well have received its baptism of fire over Cuba, during the crisis of 1962-63 centring on the supply of Soviet ballistic missiles to the island. A photograph of Camilo Cienfuegos airfield at Santa Clara taken by a Vought RF-8A Crusader on 10th November 1962 showed 'Fishbeds' with missiles under their wings', and the Soviet fighters – MiG-21F-13s – soon appeared at other locations. Had Fidel Castro and Nikita Khrushchyev not backed down, there is little doubt that these aircraft would have had to take on the whole US war machine

The first true war in which the MiG-21 took part was between India and Pakistan during 22 days in September 1965. Here the main opponents were the F-86F and Hawker Hunter, though the Pakistan Air Force (PAF) had a handful of F-104As to pit against the Indian Air Force's still quite new MiG-21F-13s. The IAF's

28 Squadron had sent their first eight pilots to the three month conversion course in Kirghizia in October 1962, the training being totally rigid, repetitive and rather boring. Instrument flying or entry into cloud was prohibited, as was use of full flap on landing or the display of any kind of initiative or departure from strict procedures.

The squadron lost two aircraft in a head-on collision on 21st December 1963. Moreover, in the early days it also suffered severe serviceability and training problems, and in 1965 only eight MiGs could be fielded at the start of fighting. They flew intensive combat air patrol (CAP) missions over two forward PAF air bases in the Punjab, but were unable to engage in combat. Thus, results were inconclusive, though the IAF learned a great deal. Co-author Gunston outlined this in one of his earlier books, *Mikoyan MiG-21* (Osprey, 1986).

These lessons were put to use when war against Pakistan resumed between 3rd-17th December 1971. MiG-21s, mainly of the FL type flown by IAF Nos.1, 4, 8, 28, 29, 30, 45 and 47 Squadrons, made numerous deep penetrations into West Pakistan but seldom were able to encounter the enemy. However, on the morning of 6th December Flt Lt S V Shah, escorting

HAL HF-24 Maruts on ground attack sorties in the Sind-Rajasthan sector, destroyed a ground-hugging PAF Chinese-built F-6, opening fire with the GP-9 gun pod from long range (about 600m, 2,000ft) at a steep angle. Thus, ironically, what is believed to have been the MiG-21's first combat victory was in effect against another MiG.

Unfortunately, to this day it is difficult to research the Indo-Pakistan conflicts. Many articles and books mention Shah's confirmed victory, yet in a day-by-day account by Indian correspondent Pushpindar Chopra in *AIR Enthusiast* for April 1972 this encounter is not mentioned.

It was not until 12th December that the engagement the world of aviation had waited for actually happened. By 1971 few PAF F-104 Starfighters were still operational, but on the night of 4/5th December ten Starfighters of the Royal Jordanian Air Force flew to Masrur, Karachi, to come temporarily under PAF command. It was two of these aircraft which, on 12th December, began strafing targets on the south coast of the Rann (Gulf) of Kutch. Flt Lts Soni and Saigal were scrambled from Jamnagar, and intercepted.

The unmistakable profile of a MiG-21 caught in the graticules of a HUD weapons sight. While this was often the case, there must be thousands of times when the graticules belonged to a MiG-21 and the outline to another type! Russian Aviation Research Trust

The VVS had little chance to use the MiG-21 in anger – thankfully. Posed photograph showing pilots walking across the vast apron to their machines. MiG-15UTI in the background.
Yefim Gordon archive

One F-104 escaped, but Soni was easily able to follow the other round in almost a 360° turn in full afterburner, at very low level. With speed rising beyond 1,200km/h (about Mach 1), Soni closed on his target. At 900m range an F-104 in afterburner looks like a tiny orange spot, a good Sidewinder target, yet Soni selected *guns*. Amazingly, he hit, and the '104 flamed. The pilot ejected. According to Chopra's diary the pilot was captured. If so, he had remarkable luck, because he ejected *downward, at Mach 1*, into a sea infested with *sharks*.

This was hardly a combat, but a lucky strike on a fleeing opponent. However, on the last day of the war, 17th December, 29 (Black Scorpions) Squadron claimed four F-104s without loss. Operating from Uttarslai, Sqn Ldr I S Bindra, the CO, took off to escort Maruts when he was advised of a lone F-104 approaching at high speed. Bindra had no difficulty in getting on the tail of the '104 and fired a K-13A missile, but this failed to achieve lock-on. He fired his other missile, and this exploded near the F-104's cockpit. Bindra then opened fire with 23mm cannon, and the target plunged into sandhills.

This delayed the Marut strike, which left after a further short briefing. Flt Lts N Kukreya and A Datta were flying escort when, approaching Umarkot, Kukreya said 'Two bogeys ahead!'. One of the hostiles launched an AAM (undoubtedly a Sidewinder), which missed. Within seconds a stern chase developed, at about 500m (1,600ft) altitude, comprising the No.2 F-104, Kukreya, the No.1 F-104 (the AAM firer) and Datta. Datta advised Kukreya to turn hard to starboard, and then found he was rapidly overtaking the F-104 in front, and that he was within K-13A firing parameters, as indicated by the

headset audio note and the radar display. He fired both missiles, and then switched to guns. Before he could take aim the target erupted in a fireball.

Kukreya broke to starboard as advised, but felt a judder ripple through his MiG. Afterwards it was surmised this may have been an engine surge caused by flying through air disturbed by gun fire from the F-104 behind, which was destroyed seconds later by Datta. Kukreya likewise found that in full reheat he was swiftly overhauling his target. The latter turned to port, from North to West, and Kukreya found he could cut off the corner and close from 5km range to 2km (3 to 1.2 miles). He fired a K-13A, which failed. After about five seconds he fired the other, and this was detonated beside the target by its proximity fuse. Smoking, the F-104 spiralled down to the ground. The MiGs rejoined the Maruts, after an action lasting less than two minutes.

On the Eastern Front the MiG-21FL operated in both air superiority and ground attack roles. Weapons were the K-13A, GP-9, FAB-500M62 bomb of 500kg (1,102lb), napalm, UB-16-57 rocket launcher and the S-24 rocket of 240mm calibre, which could be launched beyond the range of light AA fire. On the first attack mission, two aircraft equipped with guns and K-13As escorted four each armed with 500kg bombs, which made deep craters in the runways of Tejagon air base near Dhaka (Dacca). Many hundreds of 57mm rockets were fired, the US magazine *Newsweek* recording that A A Malik, Governor of East Pakistan (today Bangladesh) was 'in a state of shock', and shakily wrote his notice of resignation, after salvoes of these missiles had arrived at his residence.

Following this war, both Pakistan and India

expressed satisfaction with the aircraft they had used, but this was only to be expected. There is little point in repeating the inconsistencies and irreconcilable combat claims, but it is indisputable that the MiG-21 could always out-turn the F-104 (hardly news) and also accelerate faster and overhaul it (which was unexpected). It was the older F-86 and F-6 (MiG-19SF) that proved harder to beat, and on one occasion an F-86 shot down a MiG-21. There appears to be no record of an engagement between a MiG-21 and a Mirage IIIEP. According to the IAF, they ended the conflict with 45 losses and shot down 94 PAF aircraft in air combat, but this is not broken down by types.

To counter the claim that the MiG-21 in afterburner at low level would run out of fuel before it could go anywhere, the IAF could reply that in every inconclusive engagement it was the Pakistani pilot who broke off first. Moreover, on the few occasions when a MiG-21 was hit, it proved survivable. One aircraft, hit by AA fire (thought to have been from a quadruple 0.5in mount) over the Chamb area, returned with three large areas of damage, one series of strikes having removed fuselage skin over a region 1.22 x 0.33m (48 x 13in).

Turning to the Middle East, on 16th August 1966 an Iraqi pilot defected to Israel with his MiG-21F-13. Its new owners changed its true number of 534 for the 'James Bond' 007, in which guise it was extensively tested in Israel and the USA.

In the Six-Day War of 5-10th June 1967 the outcome was decided by the IDF/AF's preemptive strike on Arab air power at the outset. In about three hours some 300 United Arab Republic aircraft were destroyed, almost all on the ground. Few Egyptian or Syrian aircraft managed to get airborne, and only 19 Israeli aircraft were lost.

With permission, the following is taken from the co-author's earlier book on the MiG-21: 'The very first casualty of the war was thought to have been a MiG-21 of Egypt's 45 Squadron caught as it took off from Abu Sueir, and another was destroyed there minutes later as it tried to land on the cratered runway. At Inchas three MiG-21FLs of 40 Squadron managed to get airborne between the craters immediately after the first wave of attacks, one shooting down a [Dassault] Ouragan over Cairo West. After the second wave, at 1001 hours, another managed to get airborne from the completely wrecked air base and shot down a [Dassault] Mystère just outside the perimeter; but minutes later the last two serviceable MiG-21s were blasted by a Mirage IIICJ just as they reached the shattered runway...'

Arab air force MiG-21s did not fare well against the Israelis. An early coup was the defection of an Iraqi example on 16th August 1966. This was evaluated by the IDF/AF who could not resist the '007' spy-type call-sign and almost certainly went on to fly in the skies over Nellis Air Force Base. It is now in the IDF/AF museum.
Yefim Gordon archive

'...the Israeli destruction of the airfield was not yet over, because at 1030 a large group of MiG-21s and the MiG-19SFs of 20 Squadron, which had urgently flown up from Hurghada in the south, were bounced by Mirages as they tried to land. Four were shot down at once, and the rest were put out of action in trying to land on the blasted runways or in belly landings on running out of fuel.'

'On the far north east front the Syrians were in the process of converting their critically small number of fighter pilots – barely half the number needed to operate their two full-strength fighter squadrons – from the MiG-21F to PF. As the Israelis could not hit everywhere at once the Syrians escaped on the morning of 5th June, and at 1145 a dozen MiG-21PFs bombed the oil refinery at Haifa and strafed Mahanayim air base, but retribution was not long in coming. By 1300 all Syrian airfields except distant T4 had been hit, and T4 was attended to in mid-afternoon...'

'For the rest of that brief war the combined and once mighty air power of the UAR managed no more than the occasional pinprick. Almost the last MiG-21s to get into the air were two Egyptians which at 0536 on Day 2 tried to strafe the incoming Israeli army near Bir Lahfan. Both were caught by Mirages. Another (possibly the last airworthy) PF was shot down on 7th June as it escorted an [Ilyushin] Il-28 trying to bomb the occupied airfield of El Arish.'

At least one MiG-21 was still serviceable on 7th June, because on that day an Iraqi example managed to score a hit with a K-13A missile on an Israeli Mirage. This was quite an achievement, because at that time neither the Sidewinder nor the Soviet copy were the world's most reliable weapons, but on this occasion the badly damaged Mirage managed to get back to its base 400km (248 miles) away.

Sporadic combats continued, even when no 'war' was in progress. Shortly after the end of the Six Day War, on 15th July 1967, the Israeli-developed Shafrir I AAM scored its first victory, downing an Egyptian MiG-21 from a range of 1.2km (just under 4,000 ft). This missile was then developed into the much more reliable and very lethal Shafrir 2, which opened its score book on 22nd July 1969, the loser again being an Egyptian MiG-21. By the time a full scale war resumed, in October 1973, the Shafrir 2 had claimed 13 kills.

In the Six Day War the virtual destruction of the far more numerous opposing air forces by Israel was due entirely to the carefully planned pre-emptive strike, and had little to do with the qualities of the aircraft involved. Afterwards the UAR, whose principal members were Egypt and Syria, resolved to do better. Most of their

American experience in Vietnam, where the MiG-21 proved itself to be a formidable opponent, brought about a change of doctrine. Suddenly dissimilar air combat training became popular and the Northrop F-5E Tiger II very much in vogue as a MiG-21 'perform-alike'. Here, an Alconbury-based 'Aggressor' taxies out, in 1984 wearing VVS-style grey and 'Red 69' call-sign. Ken Ellis collection

losses were quickly made good by the Soviet Union, and to show the degree of integrated control which was to be achieved all the new UAR aircraft carried a unified insignia. In addition to aircraft replacements, the Soviet Union supplied enormous quantities of deadly new weapons, including improved air-defence radars, the ZSU-23-4 anti-aircraft gun and the 9M9 *Kub* surface-to-air missile.

The ZSU-23-4 was a very mobile vehicle which carried a powered and accurately radar-trained mount for a quadruple battery of 23mm guns. These were fed with belts of 1,000 rounds, sufficient for twenty 200-round bursts (50 per barrel), and as the guns were water-cooled they could fire burst after burst without stopping. The 9M9, called 'SA-6' by NATO, was guided by CW radar. Though such guidance had for decades been used for the US Army Hawk SAM, the Israelis and their American suppliers had omitted to invent any countermeasure to such a weapon, and the 9M9 was to prove as lethal at medium ranges as the ZSU-23-4 was at close range.

The UAR planned their war of revenge for 14.05 hours (2.05pm) on 6th October 1973, the special holy day in the Jewish calendar called *Yom Kippur*. The initial assault was mounted against the three biggest IDF/AF bases by 222 Egyptian aircraft, of which over 100 were MiG-21s. It went well, but knocked out only a fraction of the Israeli air power. Things then got harder, and from the following day the MiG-21s flew top cover. According to Hosni Mubarak, CO of the Egyptian Air Force and later President of Egypt, despite all their problems, air combats between the Egyptian MiG-21s and the IDF/AF tended to end in the favour of the former. For example, when on 14th October about 70 MiG-21s met a similar number of Israeli McDonnell F-4E Phantoms, the result was an 18-4 victory for the Egyptians.

The bitter *Yom Kippur* war was halted by a cease-fire on 24th October. At that time the final tally of losses was calculated by impartial (Western) observers to have been: Egypt, 223 plus 42 helicopters; Syria, 118 plus 13; Iraq, 21; Libyan and Algerian expeditionary force, 30; and Israel, 106 plus six helicopters. Almost all the Israeli losses were due to the 9M9 and ZSU-23-4. In air combat the Israelis say it was almost 'no contest', because the IDF/AF claimed 277 kills (of which 102 were gained by Mirages and IAI Neshers using the Shafrir 2) for the loss of either six or four aircraft. This hardly tallies with the Egyptian claim (supported by combat-camera evidence) of 18 F-4Es downed in a single engagement.

Co-author Gunston finds it hard to accept the Israeli figures, but as fighting in the Middle East continued, the air war certainly did become more one-sided. Though the Arab forces confronting Israel never ceased trying to re-equip with later weapons, increasingly supplied from the USA and France rather than the USSR, the IDF/AF combination of the Kfir, F-15 and F-16, using the Shafrir 2, its successor the Python

and the AIM-7F and AIM-9L, appear to have had complete mastery of the sky. In 1977-82 a carefully confirmed total of nearly 100 Syrian aircraft (the bulk being MiG-21s) were shot down in air combat by the IDF/AF without a single loss.

In contrast, fighting between Egypt and Libya in late July 1977 came out roughly even, though again what really happened is hard to discern. For example, while Egypt admitted losing just two Su-20s, Libya claimed 25 victories including seven MiG-21s.

MiG-21s continued to be involved in the Indo-Pakistan dispute, the PAF claiming that on one occasion an IAF MiG-21 mistakenly bagged his own No.2 with a missile, thinking it was the Mirage IIIEP they had been scrambled to intercept!

Upwards of 100 MiG-21s found their last resting place in the former Portuguese colony of Angola. At first the F-13 and PF versions had little opposition, but throughout the 1980s MFs flown mainly by Cuban pilots were opposed by the *União Nacional para a Independência Total de Angola* (UNITA) and *Frente Nacional de Libertação de Angola* (FNLA) opposition parties, as well as by the South African Air Force in Namibia (former South West Africa).

A number of Soviet MiG-21 units were detached to Afghanistan from 1979, but saw only limited action and proved basically unsuited to that kind of guerrilla conflict. In contrast, Iraqi MiG-21s of several species more than held their own in numerous air combats against F-4s and F-5s of the Iranian Air Force. It was the opinion of the Iraqi pilots that, despite costing less than half as much as an F-4E, the F-5 was the most dangerous opponent they could encounter.

Another region that has known little peace for over 20 years is the so-called Horn of Africa, where the principal combatants have been Somalia and Ethiopia. In July-August 1977 a succession of air battles took place in which the main aircraft involved were Somali MiG-21MFs and Ethiopian Northrop F-5As. During August Ethiopia received substantial numbers of both MiG-21s and MiG-23s, some or all flown by Cuban mercenaries, and two months later claimed to have shot down over 20 Somali MiGs for relatively light losses. See page 103 for an illustration of the graveyards of the Somali MiG-21 force.

Though bloody and bitter, so-called brush fire wars are seldom the result of painstaking analysis by major powers. In contrast, the equally bloody and bitter war in Vietnam has been carefully scrutinised, by the Mikoyan bureau as well as the Pentagon. For example, a Department of Defense study examined how the McDonnell F-4B, 'C and 'D Phantom II performed against the MiG-21PF-V.

There could hardly be a greater contrast between two jet fighters. Assumptions included a wing loading of 340kg/m² for the MiG-21 and 490 for the F-4, and thrust/weight ratios of 0.7 for the MiG and 0.8 for the F-4. Another

assumption was that turn rate at a given air-speed is governed 85% by wing loading and 15% by thrust/weight ratio, and this showed the MiG-21 to have the advantage. At Mach 0.8 – considered the most common speed in a dog-fight, though in the author's view an over-estimate – the study concluded that the MiG had a 'combat survivability coefficient' (a likelihood of winning) of 0.93 and the F-4 a figure of 0.83.

At first the aircraft were essentially all on the one side, but the conflict escalated rapidly. The arrival of the MiG-21PF-V in the NVAF (actually the Air Force of the People's Army of North Vietnam) in spring 1966 quickly resulted in the USAF adding an F-4 fighter escort to all attack missions over the North. The first aerial engagement, on 23rd April 1966, was inconclusive, but three days later an F-4C did succeed in destroying a MiG-21. This was attributed to its second pair of eyes scanning the sky, its much more powerful radar, with an effective range of 70km (43.5 miles), and the choice of the heavy medium range AIM-7E Sparrow and close-range Sidewinder AAMs. Provided it worked, the Sparrow proved highly lethal over a range up to 26km (16 miles) at altitude, falling to 7km (4.3 miles) near the ground, so the Vietnamese pilots had to work out ways of getting in close.

The Mikoyan bureau never ceased to believe that a lot depends on the fighting spirit of the pilots, and in Vietnam this made up for a considerable handicap in weapon range and an initially huge, though reducing, disparity in numbers. One technique tried repeatedly was to use MiG-17s to intercept large formations of attack aircraft at low level, where the MiG-17 was exceedingly agile. This would make the enemy formations climb to medium level, at speeds varying with type from 850 to 900km/h (528-559mph), or 500km/h (310mph) for Douglas A-1 Skyraiders, where MiG-21s in pairs would attack from the rear at 1,200km/h (745mph). They would not use their radar, and so would usually remain undetected. K-13 (R-3S) missiles would be aimed using their optical sight, and fired when properly locked-on.

In 1967 Soviet observers with the NVAF, led by aviation advisor Gen-Maj (ret) M I Fesenko, carried out a careful study of the results of air combats in the preceding year. They concluded that, in the first four months of 1966 the NVAF shot down 11 US aircraft for the loss of nine MiG-17s. From May to the end of the year a total of 47 US aircraft were shot down (confirmed by discovery of the wreckage in almost every case) for the loss of seven MiG-17s and five MiG-21s.

Occasionally MiG-21s, for various reasons, would be located in the forward hemisphere of F-4s, and then it could well be a different story. However, even the simple MiG-21PF-V packed a sting, as shown by the destruction of four Republic F-105 Thunderchiefs on 30th April 1967, three F-4s on 12th May and a total of 18 US jets for five losses in the month of August 1967. In one of the most remarkable encounters, MiG-21 pilot Kha Van Tuke shot down and

killed Col D Folin, commander of a USAF fighter wing, even though the VNAF pilot was alone and surrounded by 36 US aircraft.

When the USAF saw that its principal fighter, the F-4, was not on even terms with the simple and cheap MiG-21, except at a stand-off distance, it reacted swiftly. It ordered a wholly new fighter in the FX programme, which became the F-15. It ordered a better F-4, the F-4E, with a slatted wing and an internal gun. And it opened a special Fighter Pilot School at Nellis Air Force Base where in Red Flag exercises Northrop F-5E Tiger IIs simulated the MiG-21. (A 'black' group of real MiG-21s, of several types, were also on hand, possibly including the F-13 captured by Israel.) At almost the same time, the US Navy opened its Top Gun school at Naval Air Station Miramar, again using specially painted F-5Es as well as TA-4 Skyhawks to play the bad guys in Dissimilar Air Combat Training.

If ever an F-4 was unfortunate enough to get into a close dogfight with either a MiG-17 or a MiG-21, it was likely to be in trouble. According to the Mikoyan investigation, in the calendar year 1967 the VNAF shot down 124 US aircraft for the loss of 60 of their own aircraft. Overall, between 1966 and 1970, the kill:loss ratio in air combat was 3.1:1 in favour of the VNAF, which increasingly used the MiG-21 exclusively. Over the five years, 32 MiG-21PF-Vs were shot down. For the record, both the top-scoring NVAF pilots, Col Toom and Capt Nguyen Van Bay, were exponents of the MiG-17, armed with guns only. Both types of MiG continued to fly combat missions to the end. In June 1971 US aircraft resumed bombing of North Vietnam, and in spring 1972 a programme of 40 well-planned bombing missions called *Linebacker-I* resulted in intensive combats between F-4s and MiG-21s, the versions involved now being

the F-4E and MiG-21MF. By this time the US forces could field just over 1,200 aircraft in the theatre, compared with a total VNAF strength of 187, of which in September 1972 only 71 were serviceable, including 31 MiG-21s.

In the first engagement, two MiGs ran into 12 F-4Es and were both shot down. On 27th April two MiGs encountered a group of F-4s and shot one down. On 6th May four MiGs were met by a formation of F-4s which fired six missiles at a single MiG. The Vietnamese pilot pulled maximum g and survived, only to receive three more missiles (a total of nine), one of which hit; the pilot ejected. Running engagements on 10th May resulted in 15 close dogfights, the result of which was 7-5; the F-4s downed two MiG-21s, two MiG-17s and a J-6, while the MiG-21s bested three F-4s, the J-6s three and the MiG-17 one. On the same day MiG-21s were unable to take-off because of a force of F-4s over their airfield. A flight of MiG-17s was sent to help, and while these distracted the F-4s two MiG-21s were able to take-off, climb steeply to 2km (6,500ft) and shoot down two F-4s with R-3S missiles.

On the following day, 11th May 1972, two MiG-21s acted as decoys, drawing off four F-4Es which were hit from the rear by two MiG-21s which fired three missiles and got two F-4s confirmed. A particularly successful day for the NVAF was 18th May, when MiG-21s flew 26 combat missions, achieved eight combats and shot down four F-4s without loss. In one engagement two MiGs intercepted four F-4s and Capt Egy shot one down with an R-3S fired under high-g in a 90° bank. Battles on 12th June resulted in one F-4 and two MiG-21s being downed, but the tables were turned on the 13th when four MiG-21s intercepted a larger formation of F-4s. Two attacking at Mach 1

Angolan MiG-21*bis* parked out and suffering from the elements – note the missing panel from behind the cockpit. Mostly flown by Cubans, the type saw frequent action against rebel and South African forces.
Yefim Gordon collection

from astern broke up the formation, the other pair then downing two F-4s with missiles fired from abeam. Two more F-4s were shot down later on that day, without loss to the MiGs.

Thereafter the honours were roughly even. In an official US statement it was claimed that in July-September 1972 US fighters (of all services) in air combat shot down 17 NVAF fighters (11 MiG-21, four MiG-17 and two J-6) for the loss of 11 F-4s (nine USAF and two USN). The most successful Phantom was the F-4D (seven MiG-21 and two J-6), the F-4E scoring only three MiG-21 and the Navy F-4J one MiG-21 and four MiG-17. Of the 11 MiG-21s shot down, eight were downed by AIM-7 Sparrows and three by AIM-9 Sidewinders (none by guns).

The Soviet journal *Kryl'ya Rodiny* (Wings of the Motherland) reported an eventful training flight by an unarmed NVAF MiG-21US. In front was the Vietnamese pilot on conversion to the MiG-21, and in the back a Soviet instructor. When 8km (5 miles) from their airfield, with only 800 litres (176 gal) of fuel remaining, they received a warning of F-4s. As the first pair of F-4s made their attack the instructor took over and rolled (*bochka*, barrel) down to sea level and evaded missiles. The second pair came in in full afterburner, but the trainer, also in afterburner, turned much tighter and again survived. A third attack was also evaded, but the trainer then ran out of fuel and the instructor said 'eject!'. As they fired their seats, their aircraft was at last hit by a missile. Both men survived.

Though US propaganda often tried to give the impression that MiGs could be swatted like flies, their effectiveness is shown by the fact that when President Nixon ordered the *Linebacker-II* raids by Boeing B-52 Stratofortresses against North Vietnam in December 1972 many of the primary targets of these raids, and supporting missions by General Dynamics F-111s, were MiG airfields.

During these raids there were allegedly two engagements which were never accepted by the other side. On the first day, 18th December, when the targets were the MiG bases of Hoa Lac, Kep and Phuc Yen, a B-52D tail gunner was credited with shooting down a MiG-21, though NVAF records did not show any aircraft as lost on that evening. MiGs, both 17s and 21s, did shadow the bombers even on the darkest nights. The USAF said their task was to report the exact burst height for V750Vk SAMs.

The second strange event was that NVAF pilot Fam Tuan became a Hero of the People's Army for shooting down a B-52 on 27th December which the USAF has always attributed to SAMs. He later became the first Vietnamese Cosmonaut.

During *Linebacker-II*, while the US aircraft could operate from their huge secure air bases and carriers offshore, the MiG-21s had to be airlifted by Mi-6 helicopters from their destroyed airfields to short widely dispersed STOL strips which changed from day to day. From these they were blasted out by SPRD-99 assisted-take-off rockets brought up, with fuel and ammunition, by the same helicopters. The VNAF was assisted in these dispersed site operations by the fact that for many years they have formed part of Soviet training, and have been brought to a fine art.

The 12 days of this campaign cost the USAF a sobering 31 of the giant bombers, including 18 shot down over Vietnam. Two were downed by MiG-21s, the second falling on 28th December (the MiG-21 pilot being killed during the attack), but the MiGs were busiest in the daytime. They had eight air combats in which, for the loss of three MiG-21s, they shot down seven US aircraft including four F-4s and a North American RA-5C Vigilante. In each engagement the NVAF technique was a stern attack and hard break.

During 1972 the VNAF flew 823 sorties, 540 by MiG-21s. A total of 201 air-to-air combats took place, in which US aircraft shot down 54 NVAF aircraft (the VNAF admit losing 48), comprising 36 MiG-21, one MiG-21US, 12 MiG-17F and five J-6. They lost 90 of their own number (including 74 F-4 and two RF-4C). The MiG-21 score was 67, the MiG-17 11 and the J-6 12.

Yefim Gordon comments 'According to Russian records, which were most carefully compiled, the MiG-21 came out of the Vietnam war better than the F-4. Between 1966 and 1972 US aircraft shot down a total of 54 MiG-21s. In the same period MiG-21s shot down 103

F-4s, and many other aircraft. The F-4s alone lost 206 crew members, and of course an F-4 costs more than twice the price of a MiG-21'.

When it comes to who will win in any kind of combat, there is no substitute for doing it for real. Most of the numerical analyses have been for one-on-one engagements, which almost never happen in actual warfare (though they may be more common in future). One way to round off this chapter is to cite the figures concocted by the F-15 System Program Office (SPO) at the end of 1969 to show an uncertain Congress why they should fund the F-15 and its AIM-82A missile. It showed exchange ratios (kill/loss ratios) for engagements between a MiG-21F armed with missiles similar to the AIM-9 (ie, the R-3S Sidewinder copy) and an F-15 armed with various US missiles. The figures were: F-15 with AIM-9J, 18:1 (the F-15 would

shoot down 18 MiG-21s for each F-15 lost); with AIM-9E(X), 22:1; with the planned AIM-9K/50° (50° off-boresight capability), 245:1; and with the as-yet non-existent AIM-82/50° missile, 955:1. These figures, and others, were presented by Brig-Gen Ben Bellis, Commander of the F-15 SPO. Gen James Ferguson, Commander of the USAF Systems Command, retorted, 'Ben, if I believed your figures....we'd only need three F-15s: one in Europe, one in the Pacific and one in the US for training! Take that brief and burn it!'

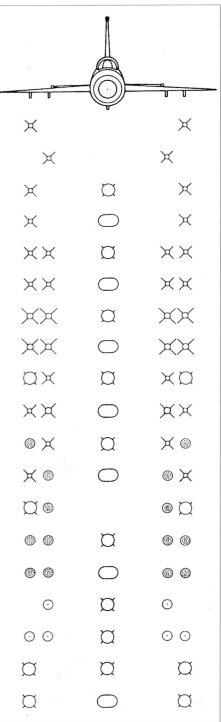

MiG-21MF External Armament Options

2 x R-3S			
2 x R-3S			
2 x R-3S, 1 x 490 litre			
2 x R-3S, 1 x 800 litre			
4 x R-3S, 1 x 490 litre			
4 x R-3S, 1 x 800 litre			
4 x RS-2US, 1 x 490 litre			
4 x RS-2US, 1 x 800 litre			
2 x R-3S, 3 x 490 litre			
2 x R-3S, 2 x S-24, 1 x 800 litre			
2 x UB-16, 2 x R-3S, 1 x 490 litre			
2 x R-3S, 2 x UB-16, 1 x 800 litre			
2 x 490 litre, 2 x UB-16			
4 x UB-16, 1 x 490 litre			
4 x UB-16, 1 x 800 litre			
2 x FAB 250, 1 x 490 litre			
4 x FAB 250, 1 x 490 litre			
3 x 490 litre			
2 x 490 litre, 1 x 800 litre			

Updated Versions

The IAI Lahav Division MiG-21 'production line' in early 1995. While nationality markings are covered up, it is thought that some of the aircraft here – which include three *Sparkas* – will be Cambodian. In the foreground is the MiG-21-2000 demonstrator/engineering model while in the background is a MiG-23 'Flogger' that defected to the Israelis. IAI

Throughout the 1980s the A I Mikoyan design bureau was kept extremely busy with major programmes, most notably the MiG-29. Co-author Bill Gunston was fortunate occasionally to talk with General Director Rostislav A Belyakov, his deputy Mikhail R Valdenberg, and most of the OKB's test pilots. On the only occasion when the MiG-21 was mentioned it was referred to as 'past history', but at the end of the decade things began to change.

In the 1990-91 *Jane's All the World's Aircraft*, the newly appointed Editor, the late Mark Lambert, opened his introduction with: 'The past year has seen an almost unimaginable change in the so-called communist *bloc* and its relations with the West. From dictatorship or one party rule to democracy; from warlike to peaceable outlooks, but also from oppression to freedom in penury; from inefficient central direction to chaotic and faltering market-driven economy.'

This perceptive assessment affected former Soviet industry from top to bottom, and no part of it more than aerospace. Almost

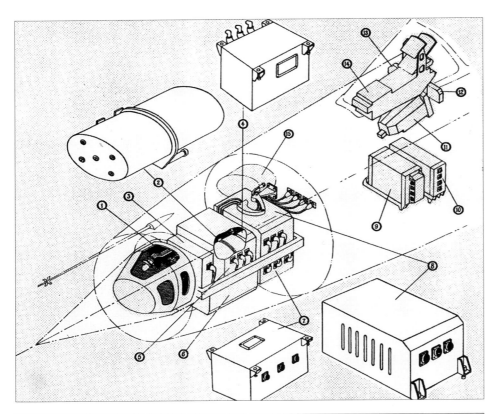

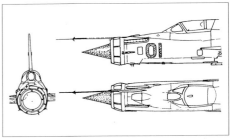

The modified inlet designed and flight tested by Kiev Military Aviation Institute, Ukraine. It finally eliminated compressor stalls in manoeuvring flight. Yefim Gordon archive

The Italian FIAR Grifo radar, as installed in a late-model MiG-21. FIAR

The first MiG-21-2000 demonstration aircraft at Paris in 1993. Robert J Ruffle / RART

overnight the old order changed. Throughout its half-century of existence the A I Mikoyan (originally MiG) design bureau had basked in the supreme confidence of having an ever more powerful position in a gigantic industry. Government funds paid for all design and development, and then – unless by some extraordinary chance the OKB was beaten by a rival, which almost never happened to the team at 6 Leningradskii Chaussée in Moscow and 6 P Osipenko St at Zhukovskii – all that was needed was to send a team of engineers to up to three series-production plants to iron out any snags while they built the resulting design by the thousand. If the OKB was good, and this team was very good, risks were minimal and rewards guaranteed.

In December 1990 the market evaporated. Suddenly, though it took time for the situation to be appreciated, the whole gigantic edifice disappeared. In future, to survive, each team had to think of products that it could sell. The good news was that it could think of any products it liked, and the new concept of konversiya positively encouraged teams which had previously produced weapons to turn to different products that appeared to call for similar high technology skills. Further good news was that they could seek markets anywhere in the world, if necessary with foreign partners. Among other things, this meant a total reorganisation.

Nobody saw the world turned more completely upside-down than the Mikoyan design

bureau. Belyakov recognised that, though the various republics of the Russian Federation were still going to require some military aircraft, this business would be peanuts compared with what they were used to. Apart from competing for a new standard advanced jet trainer, there was not a lot of secure design work for the future. Under high pressure, totally new konversiya aircraft projects were launched and new partnerships formed.

Among the partnerships one of the biggest was the formation of the Moscow Aircraft Production Organisation (MAPO). This incorporates the former Factory No.155 and the big Dementeyev plant which in the 1970s produced 500 fighters per year, and in the 1980s produced 200 MiG-29s per year. It is now scheduled to build the MiG-AT and ATTA jet trainers, provided orders are placed. With Russian government approval, in early May 1995 MAPO and the Mikoyan bureau were merged into a single company, MiG-MAPO.

Further links have been forged with the great factory which built most of the MiG-21s which in 1995 was still in low-rate production with MiG-31s. Throughout this book referred to as Factory No.21 at Gorkii, it is today the Sokol (falcon) plant in a city restored to its old name of Nizhni Novgorod. Another participant is the Novolipetsk Iron and Steel Company, which sponsored a MiG-31 to make a sales trip to Malaysia and Singapore. In the MiG-AT programme MiG-MAPO is linked with many French companies, and an assured supply of engines should result from close ties with the Moscow Machine-Building Association named for V V Chyernishov.

The first konversiya project was a multi-role transport with two turboprops in the 2,500hp class called SVB, which was later refined into the MiG-110. In addition, Belyakov and his team took a careful look at the MiG-21. Nobody had ever sold so many aircraft to so many air forces. Most of these customers had very limited budgets, which is partly why they had invested in MiG-21s. An apparent end to the so-called Cold War had no particular relevance to most of these air forces, who were going to need either a cost/effective way of updating their existing fighters or else, if they could afford it, a new replacement. One of the more difficult questions for the Mikoyan management was to decide how far upgrading existing MiG-21s would reduce the potential market for a planned successor.

The new replacement was something Belyakov's project staff had looked at for years, but they had to devote their energies to a much larger aircraft. With a number just double that of the *Dvadsat Pyervyi* (21st), the 1-42 promises to be the most agile fighter ever created, but though it is aimed at export air forces it would not be affordable to most of the customers for the MiG-21. This aircraft is important, as an essential 'Russian answer to the USAF [Lockheed-Boeing] F-22', but it is in no sense a replacement for the MiG-21. With a lower priority, the Mikoyan team also studied the MiG-33, which was, and in 1995 still is, regarded as the best successor to the MiG-

21. Again a tailed delta, it has features of the General Dynamics F-16, including a ventral inlet and a blended wing/body with the LERX continued aft to form platforms on which are mounted the airbrakes and tailerons. As this book went to press there was no Russian contract to build a MiG-33 prototype, though a low speed tunnel test model has been made.

Around 1985 Israel's IAI Lavi and Jugoslavia's SOKO Novi Avion ('new aeroplane' – specifically planned as a MiG-21 replacement) appeared to have fallen by the wayside, India – the most important single export market for the MiG-21 – was still plodding ahead with its own HAL-led Light Combat Aircraft (LCA), and Sweden (whose SAAB Gripen looked a major threat) was becoming far more eager than before to find export customers, particularly via its marketing and development tie-up with British Aerospace. In addition, the A I Mikoyan team had watched the Chinese emerge as a significant and unwelcome rival for this market, and several other companies or groups had recognised that updating MiG-21s could be good business.

As this was written, in late 1995, the Chinese had not openly announced plans for updating MiG-21s around the world, preferring to sell new J-7E and Super-7 aircraft and, with Russian help, to produce the FC-1. In contrast, several Western avionics firms have

for up to seven years been trying with varying degrees of success to get their equipment qualified in various types of MiG-21, and Western airframe companies have studied major update possibilities.

So far as can be ascertained, the first country actually to carry out an update programme was Egypt. Following the Yom Kippur War in 1973, a contract was signed with the Soviet Government under which Mikoyan carried out a major refurbishment programme of four MiG-21 sub-types then in use. In 1981, when the number of sub-types in Egyptian service had grown to nine, a comprehensive upgrade programme was planned, though in practice this was modified by replacement of earlier versions by the MiG-23 and F-16. For a start, Teledyne Electronics of the USA replaced the SRO-2 IFF installations by its digital TEC-60i, able to handle Soviet and Western frequency bands and interrogation codes. Teledyne later beat Britain's Ferranti in supplying a doppler navigation system, but GEC Marconi Avionics won a contract for the Type 956 wide angle HUDWAC, air-data computer and RWR/jammer. Tracor of the USA supplied their popular ALE-40 chaff/flare cartridge dispenser.

The upgraded aircraft were equipped to fire the Matra 550 Magic 1 missile, but in 1984 this was replaced, first by Sidewinder AIM-9P3 and from 1989 by the AIM-9L. A further 1984 upgrade was to supply for a limited number of

---

Another view of the MiG-21-2000 engineering tool/demonstrator, this time at the IAI Lahav Division. IAI

The first MiG-21-2000 on its first flight, 24th May 1995. IAI Lahav Division have transformed an agile aircraft into a formidable one. IAI

aircraft the Italian Elettronica ELT/555 jammer pod, self-powered by a ram-air turbine on the front. It had been intended to retrofit earlier versions by the Emerson Electric (now ESCO) APQ-159 radar, but the expense was not thought justified, in view of imminent replacement in the Egyptian air force by the F-16.

One of the first US companies to reach the contractual stage on upgrades was Grumman (now Northrop Grumman). In January 1987 they signed with the Pakistan Air Force to fit US engines and avionics (no details were given) to fighters supplied from China, including both NAMC A-5 'Fantans' and F-7s, and in August of that year they announced a contract worth no less than $245m from the US Air Force to design, supply and test new avionics for the Chinese F-8 II. On 21st October 1988 Grumman announced a contract with CATIC (see Chapter 11) to produce an upgrade called the Super-7. This extraordinary support of a competitor industry was abruptly terminated when Grumman were required by the US Government to withdraw from collaboration with China in 1989, following the Tiananmen Square massacre. Since then Northrop Grumman's Military Aircraft Division in California have never ceased to look for a major MiG-21 opportunity, because updating is part of their business.

On the other hand, in 1993 the Pakistan Air Force decided, with help from several foreign companies, to fit its F-7s with the Italian FIAR Grifo-L multi-mode I/J-band pulse-doppler radar. The Italian company received a contract for 100, plus options for a further 50, but has encountered prolonged problems with this radar, and deliveries (not only for Pakistan) were in mid-1995 running more than six months late. GEC Marconi Avionics made the seemingly piqued comment that its Blue Hawk radar outperforms the Grifo in almost

every respect, has several installation advantages and was fully developed by 1993. Why the Blue Hawk had not by mid-1995 become a preferred MiG-21 radar is hard to explain.

It could be that other countries try harder. For example, In France Dassault Electronique has gone flat-out to get on to the MiG-21 upgrade business. From the outset it has collaborated with Mikoyan and with the Russian state research institute for aviation systems (GoSNIIAS). It has devised a total modernisation package for the MiG-21, any parts of which can be adopted by customers. The core is EWS-21, a comprehensive threat-warning system. Operating from E through J-band, with software driven 32-bit architecture, the hardware for EWS-21 weighs a mere 14kg (31lb). It includes four passive antennas in a fin radome, a processor, night vision goggle (NVG) compatible cockpit display and a plug-in memory module. It can control the US ALE-47 chaff/flare dispenser or the latest Russian types such as the BVP-1F mentioned later. Other parts of the full package include a MIL-1553B digital data bus, a stores management system compatible with all known MiG-21 weapons, static memory flight recorders and a field maintenance system. This package is recommended by MiG-MAPO.

Two major modification programmes have been purely Russian conversions for the role of pilotless target. One, converting MiG-21PF and PFM aircraft, results in the MiG-21Ye, while the other converts the MiG-21PFM into the M-21. Design work in the mid-1960s was undertaken with Mikoyan's co-operation by the Kazan Aeronautical Institute (KAI). The radar is replaced by an inert mass (ballast) to preserve cg position, while the seat is replaced by the radio receivers and autopilot inputs to the surface power units. Illustrations (see page 95) of the M-21 show two of the sev-

eral receiver antennae, in the form of truncated cones ahead of and behind the nose gear. There is also a blister above the dorsal fin. These targets follow preprogrammed trajectories at subsonic speed, but retain their 7.8 or 8.5g manoeuvre capability.

The M-21 (*Mishen* – drone) programme will ensure that the MiG-21 continues to give faithful service to the VVS well into the next century. The prototype, call-sign '01' and a former PF was readily identifiable from additional pylon-like structures either side of the rear fuselage at the base of the fin and from a fin-tip fairing.

'Production' standard *Mishen* (example, call-sign 'Red 03') have been converted at NII-VVS, Akhtubinsk and it is thought that the programme will involve no more than 100 PFs and PFMs. On the 'production' version the antennae at the base of the fin remain, but the fairing on the fin-tip has gone, replaced by a bulbous fitting underneath the nose.

In early 1996 US company Tracor was offering a drone conversion of the MiG-21, dubbed 'QMiG-21' and was reported to be negotiating with three countries (two in the Far East, the other being the UK) over a 'womb to tomb' service including ground facilities and engineering. Five MiG-21Rs and a UM had been acquired and were under conversion.

As far as published information is concerned, by 1995 three groups remained in the running to share the MiG-21 upgrade market: IAI and Elbit in Israel, and the MiG-MAPO team themselves. There is no love lost between Moscow and Israel. In 1993 Belyakov exclaimed 'How can anyone offer a

MiG-21 update without the co-operation of the designers?'. Sadly, it must be recorded that Mr Belyakov has suffered a stroke, and the *de facto* head of Mikoyan is today General Designer A A Belosvyet. He too is a market-oriented man, determined to compete for the potentially very large MiG-21 upgrade business. His leading designer Sergei Budkevich told co-author Gunston, 'Nobody can rival the service we can offer. Our team includes Fazotron for radars and Vympel for world-beating missiles.'

Time is not on the upgraders' side. Already several major users have decided instead to withdraw their aircraft, and see if they appeal to private buyers. Indeed, MiG-MAPO themselves are studying the private buyer – and especially the air museum – market. This makes it difficult to estimate the size of the potential upgrade market, but most observers put it at 2,000 to 2,400 aircraft.

Dealing with Mikoyan's opposition first, Israel Aircraft Industries (IAI), at Ben-Gurion Airport near Tel-Aviv, have for many years toiled to make themselves a world class centre for upgrading aircraft, especially combat jets. Obviously, such work is principally concerned with avionics and weapons, but it also has to include a thorough overhaul of every part, and in particular a structural audit of the airframe. It must be added that it is in this area that Mr Belosvyet would challenge a rival's ability to offer a complete certificated service to customers. He was joined at the Paris airshow in mid-1995 by Vladimir Kuzmin, MAPO General Director, who said 'A jet owner has the right to make upgrades without any co-ordination with a designer. However, he ought to bear in mind that neither a designer nor a producer bears responsibilities for their performance, approval of certification or repair technology'.

It was to a large degree failure of the Russians to maintain these very factors that led to the Israelis eagerly filling the gap. Shraga Bar-Nissan, General Manager of IAI Aircraft Group's Lahav Division, told Bill Gunston 'When the Soviet Union collapsed, all support for MiG-21s around the world vanished. We studied the MiG-21 market, and of course found it so large that within a year Lahav had built up a total capability on the later versions, from the MF onwards. We assembled a network of suppliers, and can now offer every kind of spare part for current MiG-21 versions, which is big business by itself. We have put large numbers of aircraft back into the air, in some cases after they had been grounded for more than five years.'

In addition, Lahav division added the MiG-21 to the list of aircraft for which they have a formal commitment to offering upgrades. One customer for an upgrade was the Romanian Air Force. This had been putting out feelers to avionics companies in five countries regarding the possible upgrading of their large inventory, comprising mainly the MiG-21MF and MiG-21*bis*. Astonishingly, on 24th May 1993 Elbit Ltd, of Haifa in Israel, announced a $300 million contract with the government of Romania for the whole upgrade programme! It involved 100 aircraft, to be completely refurbished in 1994-2000.

At that time actual design and conversion work had already begun. At the Paris airshow in June of that year a former Romanian MiG-21*bis* was displayed by IAI as the demonstrator for the MiG-21-2000. On the same occasion, IAI announced that it had teamed with Aerostar SA to offer MiG-21 upgrades, together with training and support facilities, on the international market. Formerly called IAR Brasov, Aerostar, of Bacau, is one of the chief Romanian aerospace companies, which among other things had been responsible for heavy maintenance and repair of the air force's MiG-21s.

Elbit is a large 'leading edge' electronics firm. Their Corporate Secretary, Arie Tal, told co-author Gunston, 'Whereas most companies are eager to announce major contracts, we make it a firm policy never to do so. That does not mean we have no work! Experience with the [Douglas] A-4 and F-4 has taught us a strategy refined over the years enabling us to provide the most cost/effective modernisation of combat aircraft whose structures are sound but whose electronics are no longer adequate. We are now heavily engaged with such aircraft as the [Northrop] F-5, Czech [Aero] L-39 and MiG-21'.

'As we concentrate on the electronics, the customer often likes to do the work himself. In the case of the MiG-21 we put together a comprehensive package, some of it our own, such as the DASH [Display and Sight Helmet], and other parts sourced elsewhere. Integrating everything calls for great skill and experience, and this shows in our overall solution, accepted by the first customer. We have the prime contract, and are now able to upgrade Russian or Chinese-built MiG-21s to any standard required.'

Lahav's Bar-Nissan elaborated on this by saying 'Yes, of course, that customer is Romania, and it involves 100 aircraft. Though Elbit is prime contractor they buy the EL/M-2032 radar and telemetry from us, and Aerostar do the upgrade in Romania with Israeli help. But Lahav division remains the leading upgrade house, with a version called 21-2000, which is really a spectrum of upgrades of different MiG-21 versions, depending on customer requirement and ability to pay'.

Dealing first with the baseline 21-2000, not many airframe changes were needed, though it was intended that integral tankage should be provided, to obtain significantly greater internal fuel capacity for reduced empty weight. Without Mikoyan participation it is doubtful that this modification could be carried out and certified. Almost the only other modification to the airframe requiring design

Dramatically modified cockpit of the MiG-21-2000, dominated by the wide angle HUD, weapons control panel and the new HDD. IAI

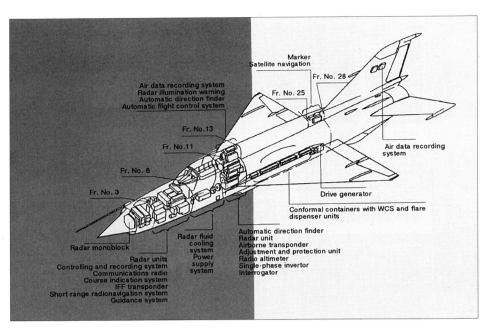

Fr. No. 28
Marker
Satellite navigation
Fr. No. 25
Air data recording system
Radar illumination warning
Automatic direction finder
Automatic flight control system
Fr. No.13
Fr. No.11
Air data recording system
Fr. No. 6
Fr. No. 3
Drive generator
Conformal containers with WCS and flare dispenser units
Radar monoblock
Radar fluid cooling system
Automatic direction finder
Radar unit
Airborne transponder
Adjustment and protection unit
Radio altimeter
Single-phase invertor
Interrogator
Radar units
Power supply system
Controlling and recording system
Communications radio
Course indication system
IFF transponder
Short range radionavigation system
Guidance system

Major elements of the MiG-21-93.
Sokol, Nizhniy Novgorod

approval is fitting a one-piece polycarbonate moulded windscreen. This improves forward view, and gives enhanced bird-strike resistance. The engine is unchanged and, apart from new avionics, the only major upgrade is the installation of a Martin-Baker Mk.10 'zero-zero' seat.

Almost all the original avionics are replaced by new technology digital equipment linked to a MIL-STD-1553B bus, which is a standard data highway common to virtually all the latest Western military aircraft. If the customer so demands, and can afford it, the radar is replaced by the Elta EL/M-2032, a member of a neatly packaged family with excellent 'look-down/shoot-down' capability (in other words, able to distinguish small targets even when they are trying to fly underneath hostile surface radar coverage, very close to the massive reflection from the ground). Against fighter type targets the look-up range is typically 65-102km (35-55nm), and the look-down range 56-83km (30-45nm). The 2032 also has doppler beam sharpening (DBS), which is a way of fooling a small fighter radar into thinking that it is a huge synthetic-aperture radar (SAR) and thus display fine detail pictures of the ground ahead. The antenna is a mechanically scanned flat plate planar array. The circuits have integrated ram-air and liquid cooling, and installed weight in a MiG-21 is about 80kg (176lb).

Bar-Nissan stressed that Lahav can offer a cost/effective radar upgrade without the cost of a new radar. 'Over 18 months we worked on a MiG-21*bis* radar in the laboratory. We extracted the raw signal, processed it in computers, eliminated false alarms and refined it for presentation. We also gave the pilot direct control of elevation/azimuth scan angle, all without losing our basic objective of hands on throttle and stick (HOTAS). With the original Sapfir RP-22 still in place, the result is an order of magnitude improvement in performance'.

Of course the radar feeds a new multi-function display in the cockpit, where there are a colour tactical display and a monochrome head-down display (HDD). Other new equipment include an advanced inertial navigation system (INS), a brilliant El-Op HUD, a single mission computer and a continuous wave (CW) jammer. The Lahav upgrade includes a mission planning centre, from where a 'ruggedised' data cartridge can be loaded into the aircraft in seconds. An Elbit DASH is an option. A new stores release subsystem is included, and two possible weapon options are the Rafael Python 3 infra-red AAM and a range of air/ground attack weapons including the long-established Mk.83 laser-guided bomb (LGB). At first there was no mention of a laser target designator, but more recent offers by IAI have included a designator carried in an external pod. Other external additions include chaff/flare dispensers, larger tanks and a choice of EW pods.

In early 1994 an Antonov An-124 'Ruslan' landed at Ben-Gurion airport and unloaded a well-worn Cambodian (Kampuchean) MiG-21*bis*. Before long it had been joined at Lahav division by seven more, as well as four MiG-21MF fighters. By spring 1995 Lahav had three upgrade contracts for over 25 aircraft. The first to be completed made a very successful maiden flight on 24th May 1995, with an IAI Kfir flying chase.

In mid-1995 Lahav was working on a $16m contract with Cambodia for the refurbishment and upgrading of 'between 10 and 20' of that air force's total of 22 MiG-21s. As already described, for reasons of cost no new radars are being installed, but the work would

improve the structure, flight safety, external store carrying and maintenance. Lahav division is also considered to be the front-runner in a planned upgrade 24 MiG-21MFs and six UMs in the Czech Republic. The prime contract would be placed with the LOK or LOM repair works, which maintained the aircraft, the IAI division being subcontractor for most of the hardware supplied. Here again, however, there is a faction recommending that the MiG-21 force be grounded. An even bigger possible deal involves up to 250 aircraft in Poland.

The other firm programme for upgrades is that by MAPO-MiG themselves, in Moscow. They are in the proverbial cleft stick, because they would much rather sell new fighters than update old ones, and each MiG-21 updated might be equated with one new fighter not sold. In any case, in their view the only MiG-21s really capable of being modified to remain competitive into the next century are the MF and its immediate relatives and the *bis*; indeed, in mid-1995 Bill Gunston was told that MiG-MAPO's opinion is hardening on the *bis* alone.

The immediate programme is to market an aircraft designated MiG-21-93, from the year in which it was first displayed in Moscow. The project got under way because the Indian Air Force (IAF), one of the Mikoyan bureau's best customers and licensees, recognised in the early 1990s that the indigenous LCA was not going to achieve initial operational capability until several years after the planned date of 1997. At first, with Mikoyan help, HAL had hoped to update IAF MiG-21s themselves. Among other things, they investigated replacing the engines by the Turbo-Union RB.199, General Electric F404 or Soviet Klimov RD-33. The IAF had stated a requirement for 200 LCAs to replace the obsolete HAL Ajeet (a licence-built and much-updated Folland Gnat single-seat fighter) and all except the latest MiG-21s. Though by 1992 the LCA was making distinct progress, the need for a new fighter grew increasingly urgent. After talking to a number of possible partners, the IAF and HAL decided to accept the proposals of the A I Mikoyan team, which had been first submitted to New Delhi in September 1991. One of these proposals was that only the MiG-21*bis* version was worth the cost of a major upgrade. The initial contract between the Indian Government (and HAL) and Mikoyan was signed in April 1993. The immediate need was to modify 100 aircraft, with the possibility that a further 70 conversions might be needed, but in May 1994 this was amended to '120 aircraft plus an option on several dozen more'.

In mid-1995 MAPO's General Director, Vladimir Kuzmin, said a contract was imminent. Indeed, it would have been signed 18 months previously, but the Indian government have been worried at Russia's soaring inflation. Unofficial reports say that the 1992 price for upgrading each MiG-21I (I – India) was

$1.5 million, but that by 1995, despite MiG-MAPO's best efforts, this had more than doubled. The Indians were even reported to be seeking alternative bids from Lahav and Elbit. Meanwhile, MiG-MAPO got on with the first upgrade, and this aircraft began its flight test programme on 25th May 1995, one day later than the Israeli MiG-21-2000. It was soon joined by a second conversion. On 11th October 1995 it was announced at the air force commanders conference in New Delhi that government approval had been given for the first $33.3 million to start the programme, which would be undertaken by HAL at Bangalore. On 24th October, however, Moscow announced that the Sokol plant at Nizhniy Novgorod had been awarded the work. (The truth may well lie between the two, with Sokol providing 'kits' and HAL the installation and flight test.)

It goes without saying that the original design team have a gigantic head start in any major upgrade programme. Any other organisation would find it difficult to do more than replace outdated avionics and equipment, leaving the vital structure untouched, whereas MiG-MAPO have no restrictions whatsoever, providing the customer can pay. They can switch to a different engine, make major changes to the airframe, and replace complete functioning systems if necessary, and then get the whole package certificated for operational use. In the past two years the Mikoyan team have put real effort behind MiG-21 updates, and can now offer a wide spectrum of options, though the big contract for India remains the immediate programme.

In general terms, MiG-MAPO's objective has been to package the radar and weapons of the MiG-29 into the MiG-21*bis*. At the end of this chapter the MiG-29 engine is also discussed, though this is not at present included in the Indian contract. The radar initially offered was the *Kopyo* (Spear), developed by Fazotron. Like most post-1992 Russian hardware, this has been specially designed for a global market, and in particular as a retrofit to the MiG-21 and other compact fighters. As the diagram shows, it is neatly packaged into quickly replaceable units, with a total installed volume of 0.5m^3 (17.7ft^3) and mass of 165kg (363.7lb), including the liquid cooling system. Though a bigger package than the Israeli EL/M-2032, this is similar to the *Sapfir* RP-22 which it replaces.

In general design the *Kopyo* resembles the same company's N-010 *Zhuk* (Beetle), fitted to the MiG-29M. With its mechanically scanned flat plate antenna housed in a radome inside the MiG-21 inlet cone, it can detect fighter size targets at ranges initially said to be around 45km (28 miles), but in late 1993 this was upgraded to 57km (35.5 miles). Its target-altitude limit of look-down shoot-down performance is an excellent 30m (100ft). Whereas the RP-22 could track only single targets, the *Kopyo* is designed to track-while-scan (TWS)

eight simultaneously, and lock-on to the two deemed to be posing the most immediate threat. It incorporates new-generation processors, and can be linked with a helmet sight. BITE is provided, and mean time between failures (MTBF) is stated to be not less than 120 hours.

At the 1994 Farnborough airshow Fazotron revealed the *Super Kopyo*, which has been developed to fit the same space as its predecessor. This radar was stated to detect front hemisphere targets at ranges from 57 to 75km (up to 46.6 miles), or tail-on fighters at up to 45km (28 miles). It incorporates a new processor, which among other things can count the targets in a group. In the improved MiG-21-93 Mikoyan also offers such optional extras as an opto-electronic unit comprising an IR search/tracker combined with a laser

range finder for directing air/surface missiles. The MiG-21-93 can also have a data link enabling a group of three to be directed to targets by a MiG-31, though this is of interest only to Russian users.

The missiles that can be carried now form an impressive group. For close combat the R-60 has been replaced by the R-60M or MK, carried in triplets, and the totally new R-73E. For engagement of aerial targets at medium ranges, customers have a choice of the 1975-technology R-27R1 or T1, or the 1985-era R-77 (RVV-AE), which outmanoeuvres any known Western equivalent. For attacks on surface targets the weapons originally offered were the massive Kh-31A (active radar) or 31P (passive anti-radar) carried on the centre-line or two Kh-25MP carried on wing pylons. In 1993 a model 21-93 was displayed with two Kh-35 long range anti-ship cruise missiles. Among many other air/ground weapons are pairs of KAB-500KR TV-guided 'smart' bombs.

One of the options offered by MiG-MAPO, especially for older MiG-21 versions, would be a low cost aircraft tailored solely to attacking surface targets, without a radar but with the latest air/ground missiles and a laser ranger/designator, or a combined pod housing TV as well as a laser designator.

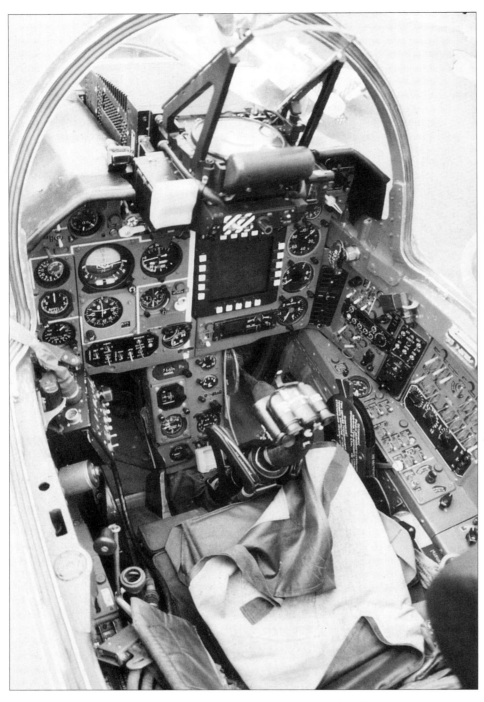

The peacock-blue MiG-21-93 cockpit has a multi-function display, HOTAS stick and Zvezda K-37 seat. Viktor Drushlyakov

In 1990 IAI Lahav studied the prospects for air/ground MiG-21 upgrades with just an Elta telemetry ranging radar (with or without a target designator) and decided not to offer such a deal, as they considered the aircraft would be too limited in versatility. In all upgrade options the GSh-23 gun is included, as well as the previous capability of carrying bombs, rockets or drop tanks.

The original MiG-21I standard included four chaff/flare dispensers installed in tandem pairs on each side of the fuselage in a long conformal fairing above the wing roots. These were of the same BVP-30-26 type as fitted to the original MiG-29, each housing 30 payloads of 26mm diameter, the dispensing sequence being controlled by a Type 20SP programmer. In the 21-93 displayed in 1993 the dispensers were of the later BVP-1F type. A customer option is a choice of Russian or French Dassault advanced RWR antennas facing obliquely to front and rear from fairings at the top of the fin.

Like the Israeli rivals, all forms of the MiG-21-93 would incorporate a frameless windscreen of bird proof polycarbonate to give an improved forward view. Unlike rivals, MiG-MAPO can certify the airframe with a life extended to 3,500 hours or 30 years. Other new equipment includes an uprated electric generating system, an INS (preferably French Sextant Avionique) with a GPS or Glonass satellite interface, new stores management, digital air data recorders, wide angle HUD (French Thomson-CSF) and multi-function HDD, digital computer and helmet-mounted sight (HMS).

Most former Warsaw Pact countries have tended to look to the West, or junk their MiG-21s, or defer any decision on what to do. Bulgaria has shown enthusiasm for participation in any upgrade programme. TEREM, the national group which among other things has maintained the country's MiG-21s, has been licensed by the A I Mikoyan bureau to carry out upgrades of any version. In late 1994 it was planning to modify six aircraft to demonstrate its capabilities. Talks have been held with HAL to explore possible involvement in the Indian programme, and TEREM hopes to be the subcontractor to MiG-MAPO in upgrading a possible 170 aircraft in Syria.

Though not immediately aimed at the MiG-21, one of the most successful re-engining programmes of recent years has been the replacement of the SNECMA Atar 9K50 turbojet originally fitted to a Dassault Mirage F1AZ of the South African Air Force by a Klimov SMR-95. This newly certified augmented turbofan is based on the RD-33D as fitted to the MiG-29M or MiG-33. Of course, the much later Russian engine has totally transformed the French fighter, offering considerably higher thrusts, much faster response to pilot demand, dramatically reduced fuel consumption, longer time between overhauls, far better high altitude relight qualities and a total absence of combat limitations, with 'carefree' handling. In addition, the installed weight is 200kg (440lb) less, despite the new engine having a self-contained gas turbine starter and electric generators each rated at 40kVA in place of 15kVA. Maximum ratings are 5.04t (11,110lb) dry and 8.3t (18,298lb) with maximum augmentation.

The SMR-95 is the result of collaboration between Aerosud of South Africa and a Russian group called Rusjet which includes Klimov, Mikoyan, Marvol and others. It has performed so brilliantly in the SAAF Mirage that it is now the front runner for re-engining not only Mirages but also MiG-21s. MiG-MAPO now offers the engine as a strongly recommended replacement for the R-13 or R-25 for operators who can afford a re-engining programme. The difference the SMR-95 would make is little short of phenomenal, though as yet, no MiG-21 has been retrofitted with this engine.

In 1995, a collaboration programme was announced between Russia and South Africa whereby local industry (Atlas/Denel) might undertake MiG-21 upgrade work for African countries, including the installation of South African avionics.

Top: **'Production' M-21 drone, 'Red 03' at NII-VVS.**

Above: **The prototype M-21 *Mishen* drone. Note fin-tip fairing.**

Right: **Close up of the pylon at the base of the fin of 'production' M-21 drone 'Red 03'.**

Below: **Another view of the M-21 'Red 03'.** All Yefim Gordon archive

MiG-21 Technical Data

Aircraft type		First flight	Engine type	Sea-level static thrust kg (lb)		Overall dimensions m (ft in)		Wing area m² (ft²)	Weight kg (lb)		
VVS	OKB			Dry	Afterburner	Span	Length (excluding PVD)		Empty	Normal loaded	Maximum
	Ye-2	1955	AM-9B	2,600 (5,732)	3,250 (7,165)	8.109 (26 7¼)	13.23 (43 4⅞)	21.0 (226)	3,687 (8,128)	5,334 (11,759)	–
	Ye-4	1955	AM-9B	2,600 (5,732)	3,250 (7,165)	7.749 (25 5) 7.149 (23 5½)	13.23 (43 4⅞)	23.15 (249.2) 23.0 (247.6)	3,500 (7,716)	5,200 (11,464)	6,200 (13,228)
	Ye-2A, 63	1956	RD-11	3,800 (8,377)	5,100 (11,243)	8.109 (26 7¼)	13.23 (43 4⅞)	21.0 (226)	4,340 (9,568)	6,250 (13,779)	–
	Ye-5	1956	RD-11	3,800 (8,377)	5,100 (11,243)	7.749 (25 5)	13.23 (43 4⅞) 13.46 (44 1⅞)	23.15 (249.2)	4,443 (9,795)	6,250 (13,228)	
	Ye-50/2	1956	AM-9Ye + S-155	2,900 (6,393)	3,800 (8,377) + 1,300 (2,866)	8.109 (26 7¼)	13.625 (44 8½)	21.0 (226)	4,401 (9,702)	8,500 (18,739)	
MiG-21F	Ye-6T, 72	1958	R-11F-300	3,900 (8,598)	5,740 (12,654)	7.154 (23 5⅝)	13.46 (44 1⅞)	23.0 (247.6)	4,819 (10,624)	6,850 (15,101)	8,376 (18,466)
MiG-21F-13	Ye-6, 74	1959	R-11F-300	3,900 (8,598)	5,740 (12,654)	7.154 (23 5⅝)	13.46 (44 1⅞)	23.0 (247.6)	4,871 (10,739)	6,915 (15,245)	8,625 (19,015)
MiG-21PF	Ye-7, 75, 76	1960	R-11F2-300	3,950 (8,708)	6,120 (13,492)	7.154 (23 5⅝)	14.10 (46 3⅛)	23.0 (247.6)	5,256 (11,587)	7,750 (17,086)	8,770 (19,334)
MiG-21U	Ye-6U, 66	1960	R-11F-300	3,900 (8,598)	5,740 (12,654)	7.154 (23 5⅝)	13.46 (44 1⅞)	23.0 (247.6)	5,195 (11,453)	7,800 (17,196)	
	Ye-8/1	1962	R-21F	4,700 (10,362)	7,200 (15,873)	7.154 (23 5⅝)	14.90 (48 10⅝)	23.0 (247.6)	5,105 (11,254)	6,800 (14,991)	8,200 (18,078)
MiG-21PFM	Ye-7, 94	1963	R-11F2S-300	3,900 (8,598)	6,175 (13,613)	7.154 (23 5⅝)	14.10 (46 3⅛)	23.0 (247.6)	5,383 (11,867)	7,820 (17,240)	9,080 (20,018)
MiG-21R	94R	1964	R-11F2S-300	3,900 (8,598)	6,175 (13,613)	7.154 (23 5⅝)	14.10 (46 3⅛)	23.0 (247.6)	5,696 (12,557)	8,100 (17,857)	9,200 (20,282)
MiG-21S	Ye-7S, 95	1964	R-11F2S-300	3,900 (8,598)	6,175 (13,613)	7.154 (23 5⅝)	14.10 (46 3⅛)	23.0 (247.6)	5,650 (12,456)	8,150 (17,967)	9,100 (20,062)
MiG-21PD	23-31	1966	R-13F-300 + RD-36-35	4,070 (8,973)	6,490 (14,308) + 2 x 2,350 (5,180)	7.765 (25 5¾)	14.72 (48 3½)	26.5 (285)			–
MiG-21SM	15	1967	R-13-300	4,070 (8,973)	6,490 (14,308)	7.154 (23 5⅝)	14.185 (46 6½)	23.0 (247.6)	5,998 (13,223)	8,300 (18,298)	9,400 (20,723)
MiG-21M	96	1968	R-11F2SK-300	3,900 (8,598)	6,175 (13,613)	7.154 (23 5⅝)	14.10 (46 3⅛)	23.0 (247.6)	5,950 (13,117)	8,950 (19,731)	9,400 (20,723)
MiG-21I	21-31/1, Analog	1968	R-13-300	4,070 (8,973)	6,490 (14,308)	8.150 (26 8⅞)	14.70 (48 2¾)	41.1 (442)		8,750 (19,290)	–
MiG-21I	21-31/2, Analog	1969	R-13-300	4,070 (8,973)	6,490 (14,308)	8.150 (26 8⅞)	14.70 (48 2¾)	43.0 (463)		8,750 (19,290)	–
MiG-21US	68	1967	R-11F2S-300	3,900 (8,598)	6,175 (13,613)	7.154 (23 5⅝)	13.46 (44 1⅞)	23.0 (247.6)	5,380 (11,861)	8,000 (17,637)	
MiG-21MF	96F	1970	R-13-300	4,070 (8,973)	6,490 (14,308)	7.154 (23 5⅝)	14.10 (46 3⅛)	23.0 (247.6)	5,350 (11,795)	8,212 (18,104)	9,661 (21,299)
MiG-21SMT	50	1970	R-13-300	4,070 (8,973)	6,490 (14,308)	7.154 (23 5⅝)	14.10 (46 3⅛)	23.0 (247.6)	5,700 (12,566)	8,900 (19,621)	10,100 (22,266)
MiG-21*bis*	7*bis*, 75	1971	R-25-300	4,100 (9,039)	7,100 (15,653)	7.154 (23 5⅝)	14.10 (46 3⅛)	23.0 (247.6)	5,895 (12,966)	8,725 (12,966)	10,420 (22,972)
MiG-21UM	69	1971	R-11F2S-300	3,900 (8,598)	6,175 (13,613)	7.154 (23 5⅝)	13.46 (44 1⅞)	23.0 (247.6)	5,380 (11,861)	8,000 (17,637)	
MiG-21I	21-93	1992	R-25-300	4,100 (9,039)	7,100 (15,653)	7.154 (23 5⅝)	14.10 (46 3⅛)	23.0 (247.6)		8,825 (19,455)	

Aircraft type		Maximum speed optimum height		Time to climb to height	Service ceiling	Range	Ground run m (ft)		Armament	Design load factor	ASCC operating name
VVS	OKB	km/h (mph)	Mach	km (ft) in min	km (ft)	km (miles)	Take off	Landing			
	Ye-2	1,920 (1,193)	1.8		19.0 (62,336)	1,220 (758)	700 (2,297)	800 (2,625)	Two NR-30	7.0	Faceplate
	Ye-4	1,296 (805)	1.22	5.0 in 1.6	16.4 (53,800)	1,120 (700)			Two NR-30	7.0	Fishbed
	Ye-2A, 63	1,900 (1,181)	1.79	10.0 in 4.3	18.0 (59, 050)	1,400 (870)		900 (2,953)	Two NR-30	7.0	Faceplate
	Ye-5	1,970 (1,224)	1.85	5.0 in 1.6	17.65 (57,900)	1,330 (826)	730 (2,395)	890 (2,920)	Two NR-30	7.0	Fishbed
	Ye-50/2	2,460 (1,529)	2.32	20.0 in 9.4	23.0 (75,460)	450 (280)	900 (2,953)	860 (2,822)	Two NR-30	7.0	–
MiG-21F	Ye-6T, 72	2,175 (1,352)	2.04	5.0 in 2.0 18.5 in 7.5	19.0 (62,340)	1,520 (945)	900 (2,953)	800 (2,625)	Two NR-30, two UB-16-57 or FAB-500	7.0	Fishbed-B
MiG-21F-13	Ye-6, 74	2,175 (1,352)	2.04	5.0 in 2.5	19.0 (62,340)	1,420 (882)	900 (2,953)	900 (2,953)	One NR-30, Two R-3S (K-13) or UB-16-57	7.0	Fishbed-B
MiG-21PF	Ye-7, 75, 76	2,175 (1,352)	2.04	10.0 in 6.2	19.0 (62,340)	1,900* (1,180)	900 (2,953)	850 (2,789)	Two R-3S (K-13)	7.8	Fishbed-D
MiG-21U	Ye-6U, 66	2,175 (1,352)	2.04	17.8 in 8.0	18.3 (60,040)	1,220 (758)	900 (2,953)	800 (2,625)	One A-12.7, two R-3S	7.0	Mongol
	Ye-8/1	2,230 (1,386)	2.1	18.0 in 5.9	20.3 (66,600)		835 (2,740)	850 (2,789)	Two R-3S		–
MiG-21PFM	Ye-7, 94	2,230 (1.386)	2.1	18.5 in 8.0	19.0 (62,340)	1,670* (1,038)	900 (2,953)	950 (3,120)	GP-9 plus two R-3S	8.5	Fishbed-F
MiG-21R	94R	1,700† (1,056)	1.6	14.6 in 8.5	15.1 (49,540)	1,600** (994)	900 (2,953)	550‡ (1,804)	Two R-3S	6.0	Fishbed-N
MiG-21S	Ye-75, 95	2,230 (1,386)	2.1	17.5 in 8.5	18.0 (59,050)	1,240 (771)	900 (2,953)	550‡ (1,804)	GP-9s plus two/four R-3S or UB/FAB	8.5	Fishbed-H
MiG-21PD	23-31	c600 (373)	–	–	–	c1,000 (620)	300?	100?	–		Fishbed-G
MiG-21SM	15	2,230 (1,386)	2.1	17.5 in 9.0	18.0 (59,050)	1,240 (771)	900 (2,953)	550‡ (1,804)	GSh-23L plus two R-3S and two R-3R	8.5	Fishbed-H
MiG-21M	96	2,230 (1,386)	2.1	16.8 in 9.0	17.3 (56,760)	1,050 (652)	900 (2,953)	550‡ (1,804)	GSh-23L plus four R-3 or UB/FAB	8.5	Fishbed-J
MiG-21I	21-31/1, Analog	2,500 (1,553)	2.35		20+	c1,800 (1,120)	600 (1,970)	800 (2,625)	–	6.0	–
MiG-21I	21-31/2, Analog	2,500 (1,553)	2.35		20+	c1,800 (1,120)	600 (1,970)	800 (2,625)	–	6.0	–
MiG-21US	68	2,175 (1,352)	2.04	17.2 in 8.0	17.7 (58,070)	1,210 (752)	900 (2,953)	550‡ (1,804)	A-12.7, two R-3S	7.0	Mongol-B
MiG-21MF	96F	2,230 (1,386)	2.1	17.7 in 9.0	18.2 (59,710)	1,300 (808)	800 (2,625)	550‡ (1,804)	GSh-23L, two R-3S and two R-3R	8.5	Fishbed-J
MiG-21SMT	50	2,175 (1,352)	2.04	16.8 in 9.0	17.3 (56,760)	1,300 (808)	950 (3,120)	550‡ (1,804)	Gsh-23L, two R-3S and two R-3R	8.5	Fishbed-K
MiG-21*bis*	7*bis*, 75	2,175 (1,352)	2.04	17.0 in 8.5	17.8 (58,400)	1,225 (761)	830 (2,725)	550‡ (1,804)	Gsh-23L, two R-3M or R-55 and four R-60	8.5	Fishbed-L, -N
MiG-21UM	69	2,175 (1,352)	2.04	16.8 in 8.0	17.3 (56,760)	1,210 (752)	900 (2,953)	550‡ (1,804)	A-12.7, two R-3S	7.0	Mongol-B
MiG-21I	21-93	2,175 (1,352)	2.04		17.3 (56,760)	1,210 (752)			Gsh-23L, two R-27 (R1 or T1) and four R-73	8.5	–

* External tank, ** two tanks, † limited by external pod, ‡ with SPS

MiG-21s in Colour

While black and white photographs of most of the MiG-21 prototypes have been in print before, colour from the same era is very rare. The large wing fences and a look at the shadow reveal this to be the swept-wing Ye-2A. Yefim Gordon archive

The Ye-6U/1, first of the two-seaters. Yefim Gordon archive

'Red 82', the second Ye-8 with almost certainly Fedotov in the cockpit. Yefim Gordon archive

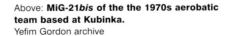

Top: **MiG-21SM with UB-16-57 rocket pods.**
Yefim Gordon archive

Above: **MiG-21bis of the the 1970s aerobatic team based at Kubinka.**
Yefim Gordon archive

Below left: **Air to air study of a MiG-21UM.**
Yefim Gordon archive

Photographs on the opposite page:

Bottom right: **An SMT, preserved in Sweden. The three-colour upper surface camouflage and yellow call-sign are evident.** Pär-Erik Nordin

Bottom left: **A view of a 1989 prototype, an un-known MiG-21 version, probably the so-called 'MiG-21K'. The aircraft was involved in the test-ing of a new or improved radar. Note the cable fairing, which is carrying trunking from the radar, rearwards over the call-sign 'Red 44' on the nose.** Yefim Gordon

Top: **A Ukrainian MiG-21SM, prior to the application of national markings. The nose decoration is of interest: some aircraft with similar eyes were deployed into Afghanistan.** Yefim Gordon archive

Above: **A UM parked on what would be called pierced-steel plating (PSP) in the West, at Akhtyubinsk in June 1995. The eagle motif is worn by several NII-VVS aircraft.** Yefim Gordon

Above: **East German Air Force MiG-21PFM.**
via Jay Miller

Left: **'United' German MiG-21bis 24+22.**
Yefim Gordon collection

Below: **German Luftwaffe MiG-21MF in 'celebratory' colours for the wind-down of JG-1's MiGs. Not only has the nose received 'shark's mouth' treatment, but the wing drop tanks have a more accurate shark eyes, teeth and gills!** Yefim Gordon archive

Top: **MiG-21PFM of the *Polskie Wojska Lotnicze.*** Yefim Gordon archive

Below left: **PWL MiG-21MF.** Waclaw Holys

Below right: **PWL MiG-21MF.** Waclaw Holys

Bottom: **PWL MiG-21R.** Waclaw Holys

Top: **Slovakian MiG-21MF 7714.** Russian Aviation Research Trust

Bottom left: **Special paint scheme on a Czech Republic MiG-21UM.** Ryszard Jaxa-Malachowski

Above: **Air-to-air of another specially-painted Czech example, in this case MF 7711.** Russian Aviation Research Trust

Bottom right: **Rear view of Romanian MiG-21U 1120. Note the marshaller using flags.** Yefim Gordon archive

Above: **MiG-21bis of the Afghanistan Army Air Force. Pictured in Pakistan, with a fellow Sukhoi Su-22M-4 'Fitter' behind, both had defected.**
Peter Steinemann - Skyline APA

Right: **The distinctive bulge below the cockpit denotes an Egyptian MiG-21RF, in this case serial number 8502.** Russian Aviation Research Trust.

Below: **MiG-21bis MG-116 of Finland's *HäLv* 31. Note small roundel and serial number.** Yefim Gordon

Bottom left: **MiG-21MF 224 (with SIAI-Marchetti SF.260WS Warrior behind) derelict at Mogadishu, Somalia. The crude painting on the nose presumably stands for 'Air Force Explosive Ordnance Disposal'.** Paul A Jackson

Bottom right: **Roman and Arabic serial number on nose and tail of a Sudanese MiG-21MF.** A J Walg – Aero Mapho archive

Above: **Missile-armed Ye-6T/3 showing its canards.** Yefim Gordon archive

Right: **View of the Ye-6T/3 from above.** Yefim Gordon archive

Below: **Ye-6V/2 receiving attention. The fairing for the parabrake under the fin/rudder is apparent.** Yefim Gordon archive

Above: **The Ye-6V/2 with take-off rocket booster installation under the rear fuselage, port and starboard.** Yefim Gordon archive

Above: **Rear view of the Ye-6V/2. The sprung tailwheel can be seen extended from the rear fuselage strake.** Yefim Gordon archive

Above: **View from above of the Ye-7/1 interceptor prototype, 'Red 71'.** Yefim Gordon archive

Above: **'Red 72', the second interceptor prototype, Ye-7/2,** Yefim Gordon archive

Above: **The Ye-7/8, prototype for the MiG-21R.** Yefim Gordon archive

Above: **Production series Ye-7, the first of the MiG-21PFs, at LII-VVS, Zhukovskii.** Yefim Gordon archive

Above: **Ye-6U/1 the prototype *Sparka*.** Yefim Gordon archive

Left, above and below left: **Three views of the so-called 'MiG-21PD' – the Type 23-31. Undercarriage was fixed.** Yefim Gordon archive

Above: **The Ye-8/1. Note the twin auxiliary inlet doors are open.** Yefim Gordon archive

Above: **The 23-31, sectioned and stripped and in use in the Moscow Aviation and Technological Institute.** Yefim Gordon archive

Left and above: **Two views of the Ye-8/2.** Yefim Gordon archive

Ye-2, swept-wing prototype.

Ye-2A, swept-wing with pronounced wing fences.

Ye-2/6 - sixth prototype.

Ye-2A (so-called 'MiG-23') with special markings for canopy jettison testing.

Ye-4 delta, fitted with RD-9Ye engine.

Ye-4 as refitted with RD-9I engine.

Ye-5, the third delta airframe, powered by the RD-11.

Ye-50-3 mixed-power interceptor.

Drawings by Vladimir Klimov

117

Ye-2A

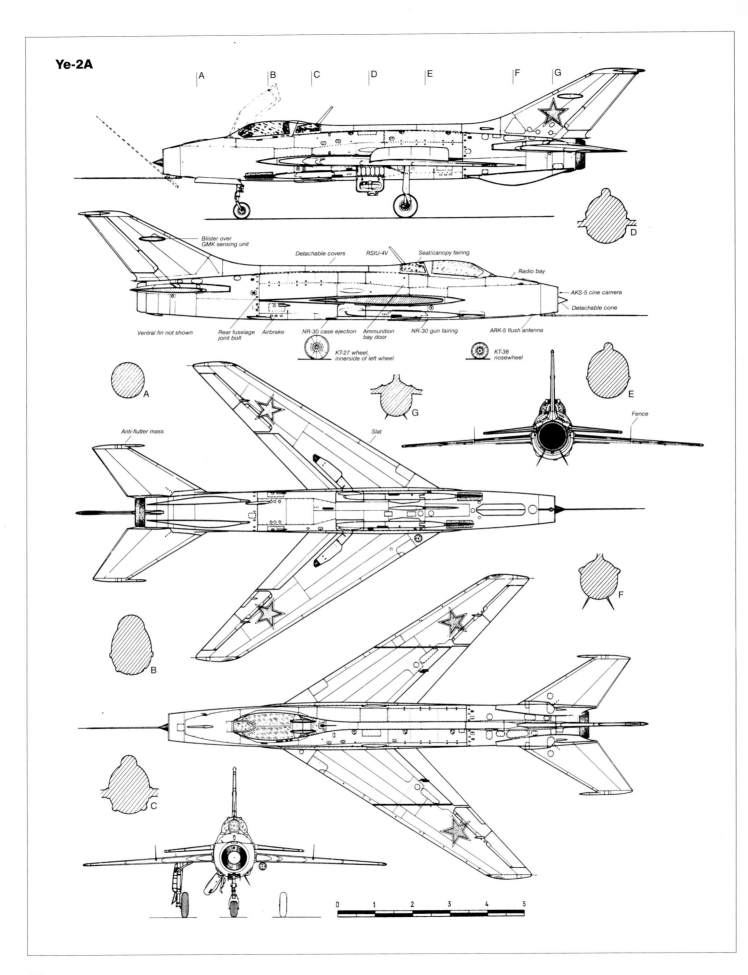

Blister over
GMK sensing unit

Detachable covers

RSIU-4V

Seat/canopy fairing

Radio bay

AKS-5 cine camera

Detachable cone

Ventral fin not shown

Rear fuselage
joint bolt

Airbrake

NR-30 case ejection

Ammunition
bay door

NR-30 gun fairing

ARK-5 flush antenna

KT-27 wheel,
innerside of left wheel

KT-38
nosewheel

Anti-flutter mass

Slat

Fence

A

B

C

D

E

F

G

0   1   2   3   4   5

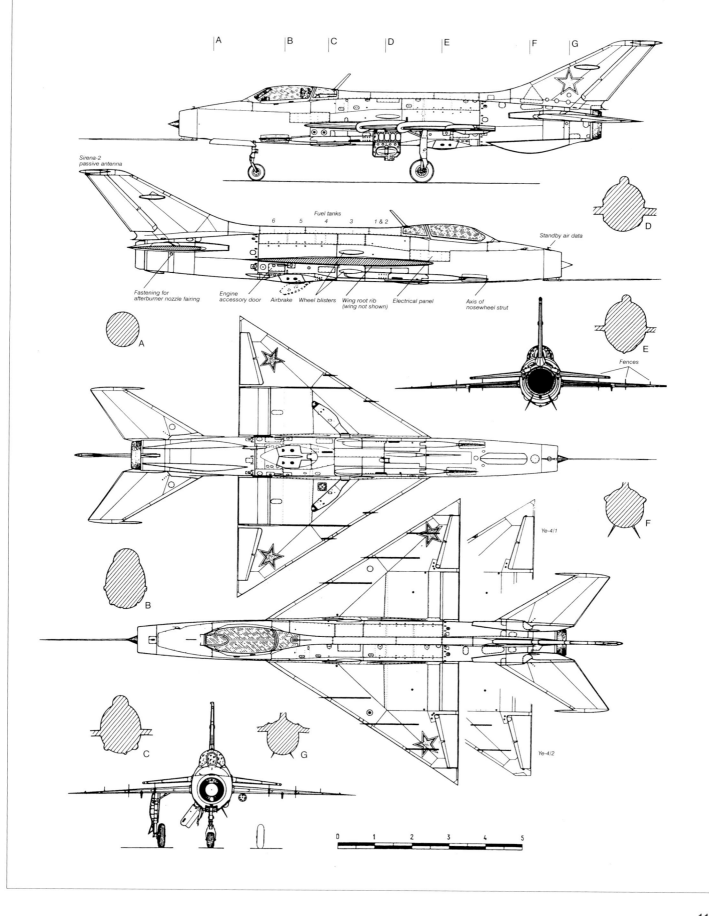

Sirena-2
passive antenna

Fuel tanks

6   5   4   3   1 & 2

Standby air data

D

Fastening for
afterburner nozzle fairing

Engine
accessory door

Airbrake   Wheel blisters

Wing root rib
(wing not shown)

Electrical panel

Axis of
nosewheel strut

A

E

Fences

Ye-4/1

F

B

C   G

Ye-4/2

0   1   2   3   4   5

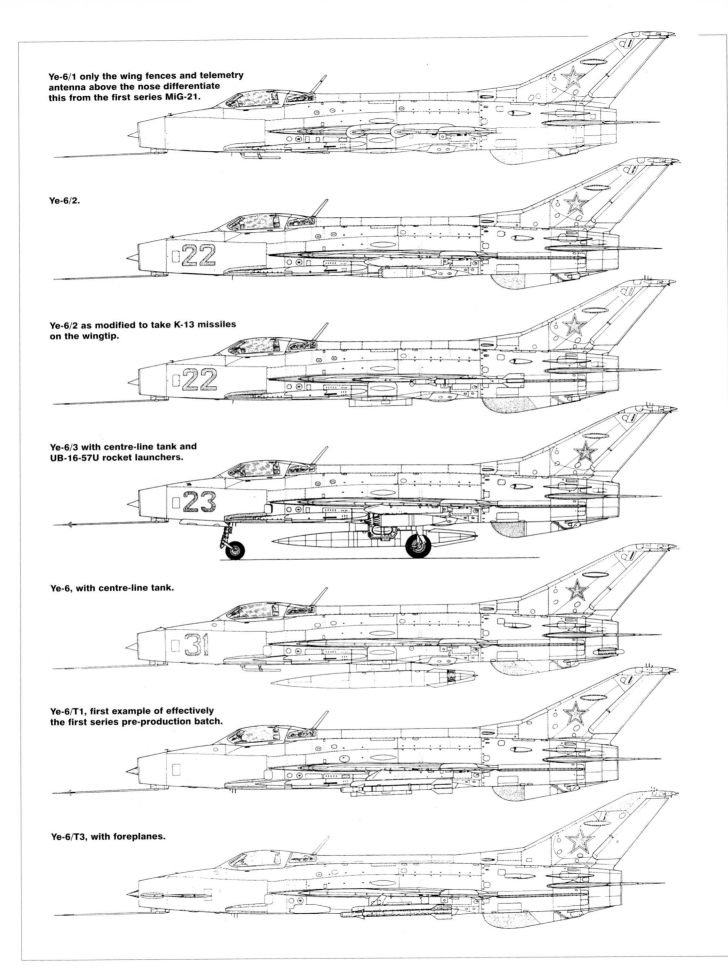

Ye-6/1 only the wing fences and telemetry antenna above the nose differentiate this from the first series MiG-21.

Ye-6/2.

Ye-6/2 as modified to take K-13 missiles on the wingtip.

Ye-6/3 with centre-line tank and UB-16-57U rocket launchers.

Ye-6, with centre-line tank.

Ye-6/T1, first example of effectively the first series pre-production batch.

Ye-6/T3, with foreplanes.

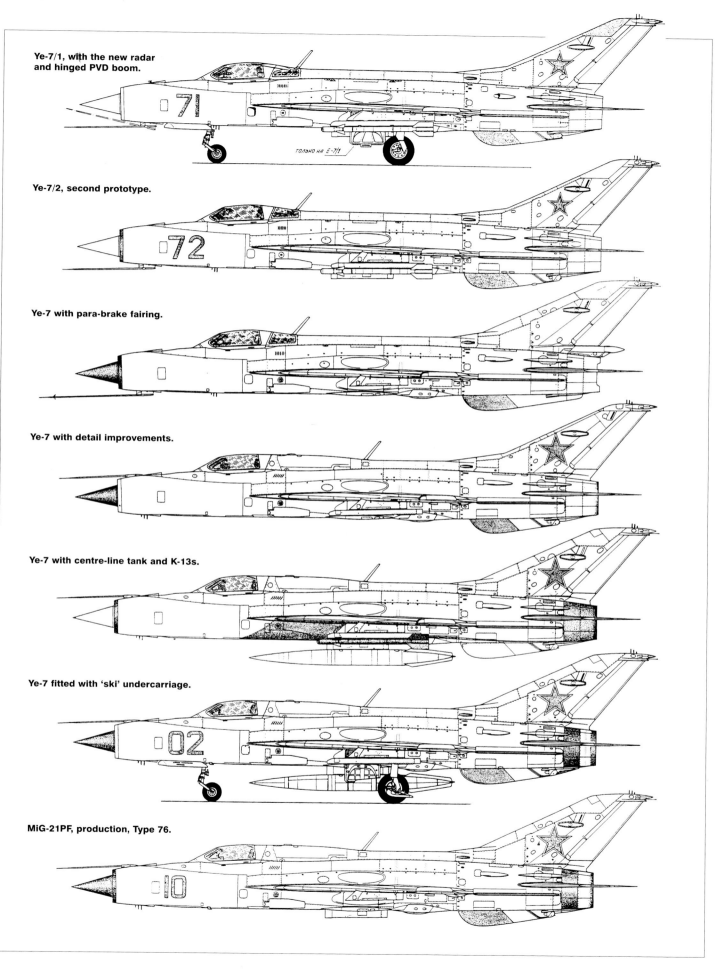

Ye-7/1, with the new radar and hinged PVD boom.

Ye-7/2, second prototype.

Ye-7 with para-brake fairing.

Ye-7 with detail improvements.

Ye-7 with centre-line tank and K-13s.

Ye-7 fitted with 'ski' undercarriage.

MiG-21PF, production, Type 76.

121

Ye-2A

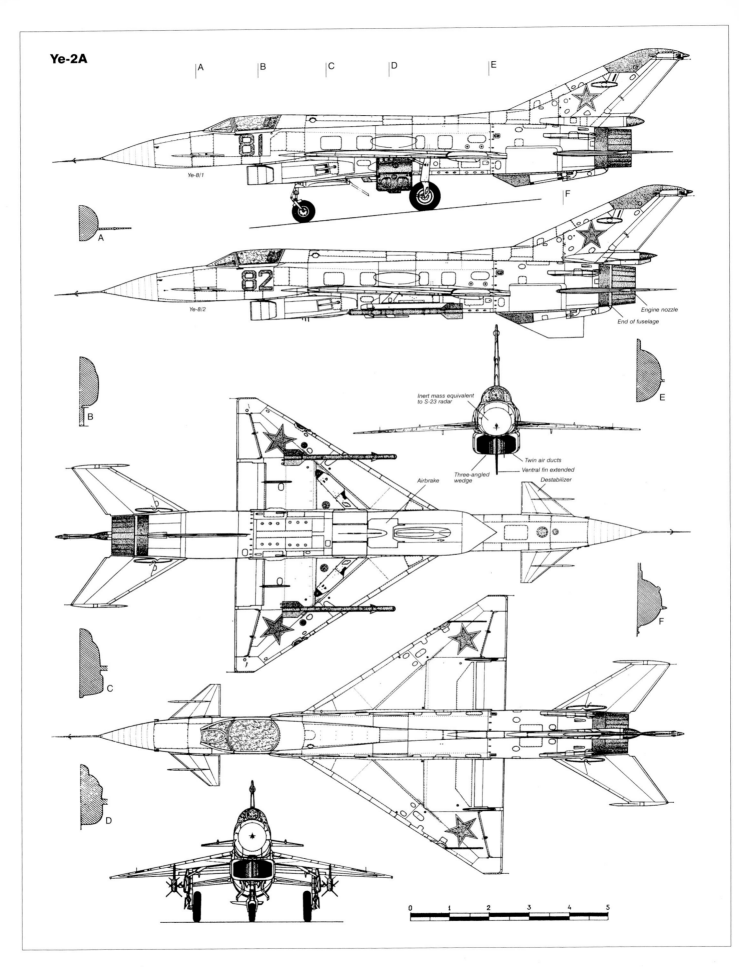

A   B   C   D   E

Ye-8/1

Ye-8/2

Engine nozzle

End of fuselage

A

B

E

Inert mass equivalent
to S-23 radar

Airbrake

Three-angled
wedge

Twin air ducts

Ventral fin extended

Destabilizer

C

F

D

0   1   2   3   4   5

Ye-50

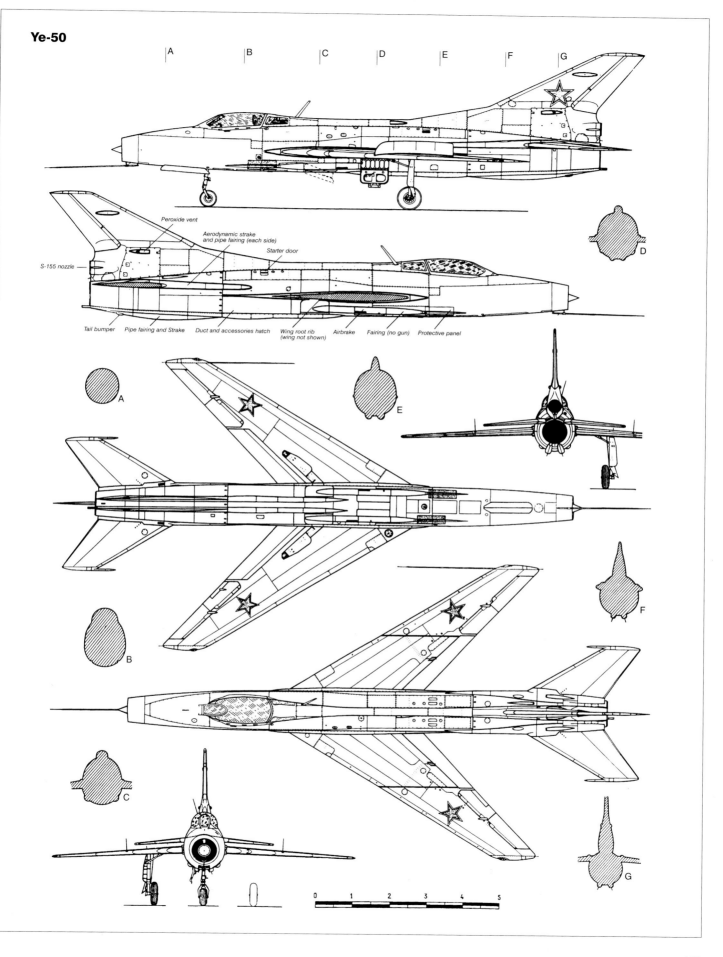

A | B | C | D | E | F | G

Peroxide vent

Aerodynamic strake
and pipe fairing (each side)

Starter door

S-155 nozzle

Tail bumper | Pipe fairing and Strake | Duct and accessories hatch | Wing root rib (wing not shown) | Airbrake | Fairing (no gun) | Protective panel

A

D

E

B

C

F

G

0 1 2 3 4 5

MiG-21PD

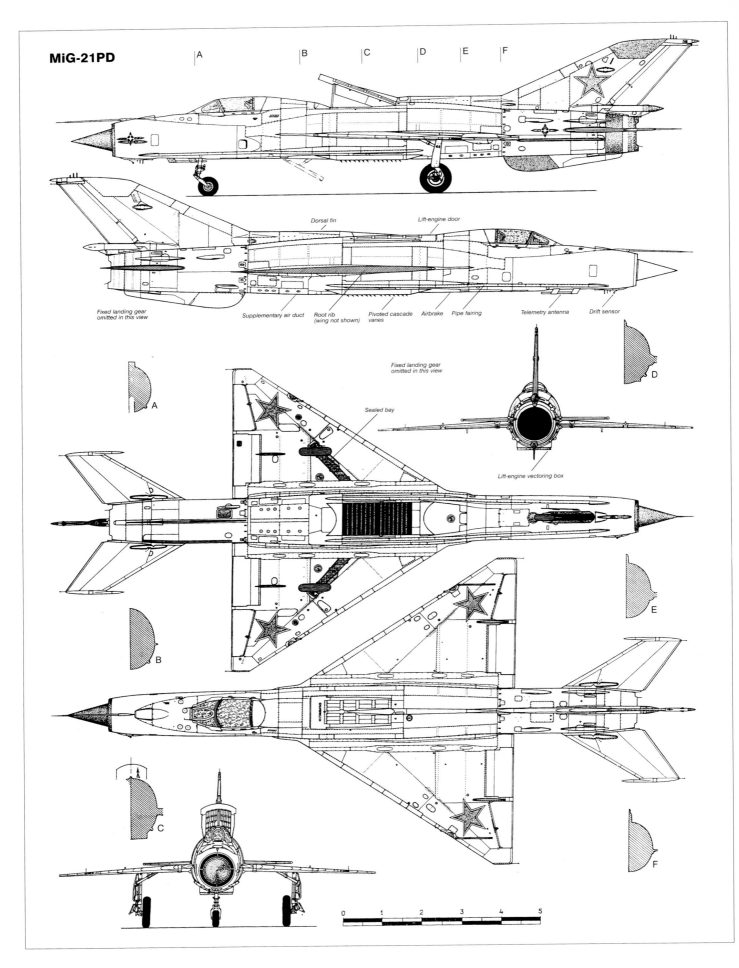

A　B　C　D　E　F

Dorsal fin

Lift-engine door

Fixed landing gear
omitted in this view

Supplementary air duct　Root rib
(wing not shown)　Pivoted cascade
vanes　Airbrake　Pipe fairing　Telemetry antenna　Drift sensor

A

B

Sealed bay

Fixed landing gear
omitted in this view

D

Lift-engine vectoring box

E

C

F

0　1　2　3　4　5

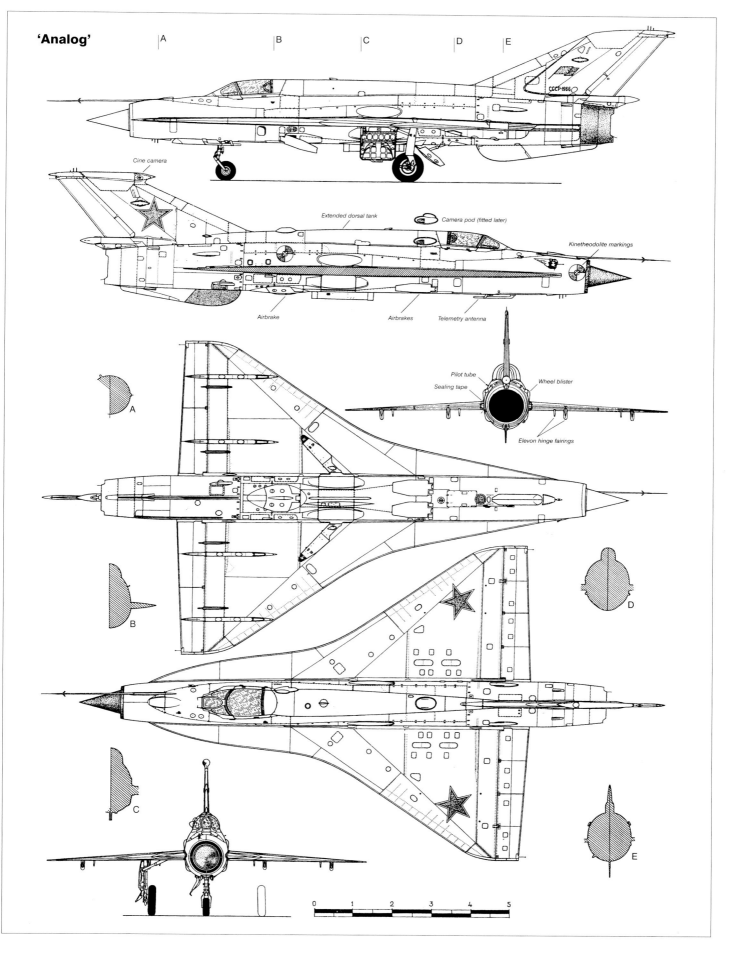

'Analog'

Cine camera

Extended dorsal tank

Camera pod (fitted later)

Kinetheodolite markings

Airbrake

Airbrakes

Telemetry antenna

Pilot tube

Wheel blister

Sealing tape

Elevon hinge fairings

A

B

C

D

E

0   1   2   3   4   5

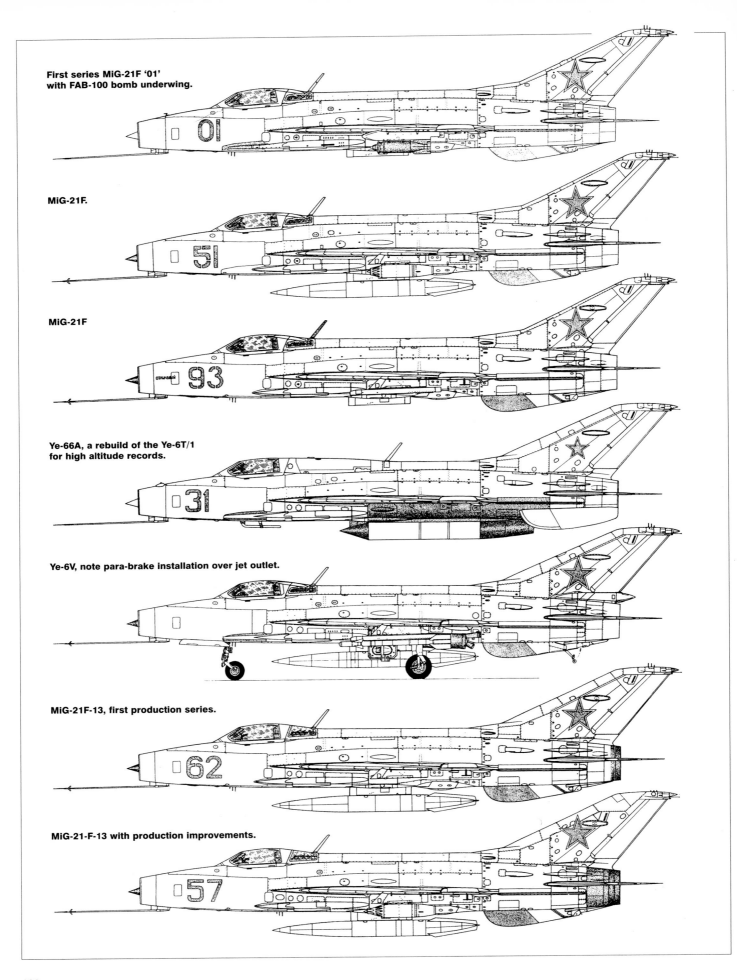

First series MiG-21F '01'
with FAB-100 bomb underwing.

MiG-21F.

MiG-21F

Ye-66A, a rebuild of the Ye-6T/1
for high altitude records.

Ye-6V, note para-brake installation over jet outlet.

MiG-21F-13, first production series.

MiG-21-F-13 with production improvements.

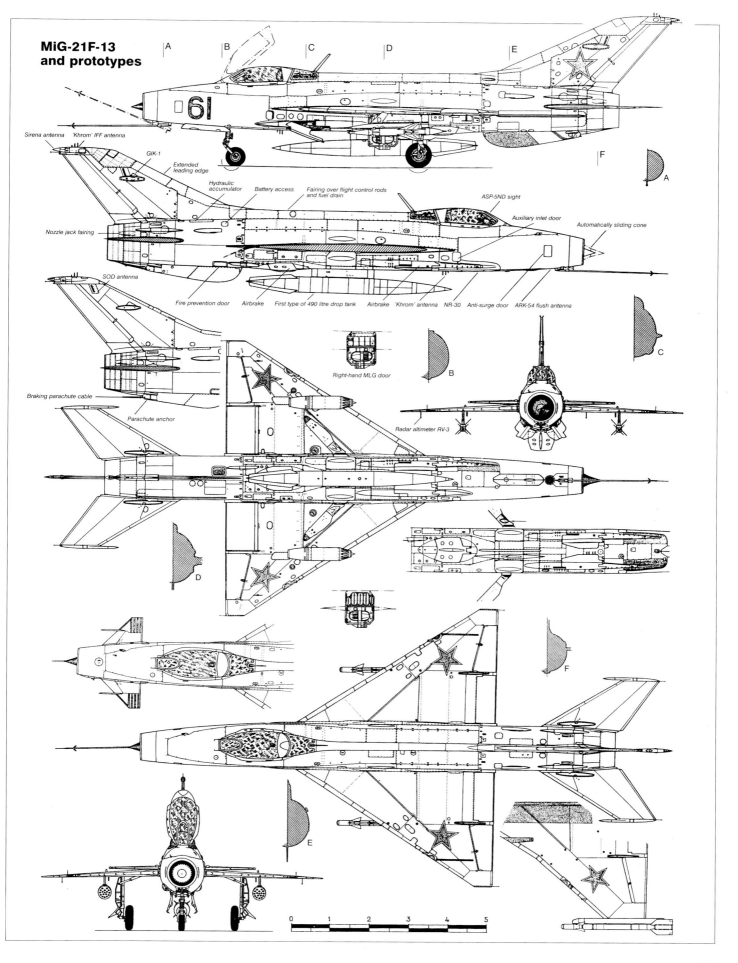

MiG-21F-13 and prototypes

Sirena antenna
'Khrom' IFF antenna
GIK-1
Extended leading edge
Hydraulic accumulator
Battery access
Fairing over flight control rods and fuel drain
ASP-5ND sight
Auxiliary inlet door
Automatically sliding cone
Nozzle jack fairing
SOD antenna
Braking parachute cable
Parachute anchor
Fire prevention door
Airbrake
First type of 490 litre drop tank
Airbrake
'Khrom' antenna
NR-30
Anti-surge door
ARK-54 flush antenna
Right-hand MLG door
Radar altimeter RV-3

A
B
C
D
E
F

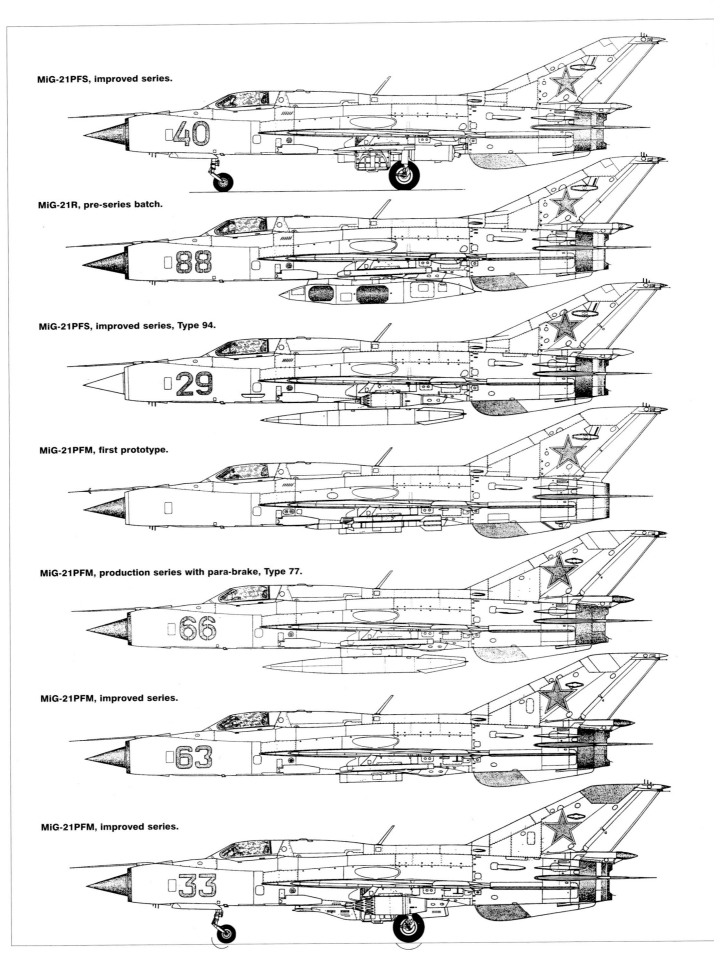

MiG-21PFS, improved series.

MiG-21R, pre-series batch.

MiG-21PFS, improved series, Type 94.

MiG-21PFM, first prototype.

MiG-21PFM, production series with para-brake, Type 77.

MiG-21PFM, improved series.

MiG-21PFM, improved series.

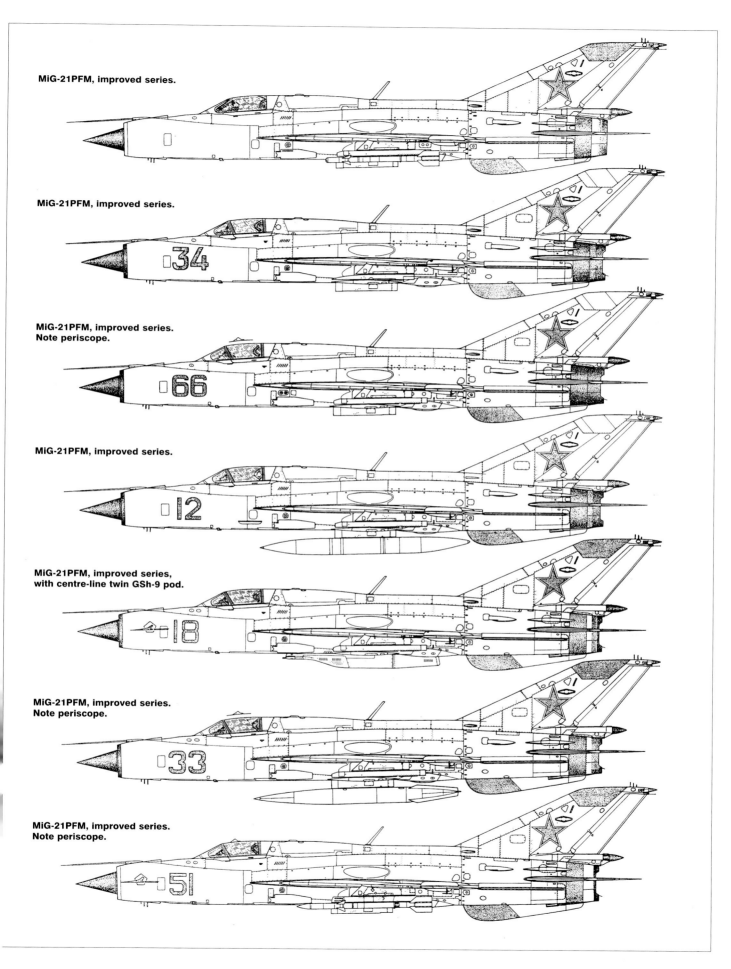

MiG-21PFM, improved series.

MiG-21PFM, improved series.

MiG-21PFM, improved series.
Note periscope.

MiG-21PFM, improved series.

MiG-21PFM, improved series,
with centre-line twin GSh-9 pod.

MiG-21PFM, improved series.
Note periscope.

MiG-21PFM, improved series.
Note periscope.

MiG-21PFM and prototypes

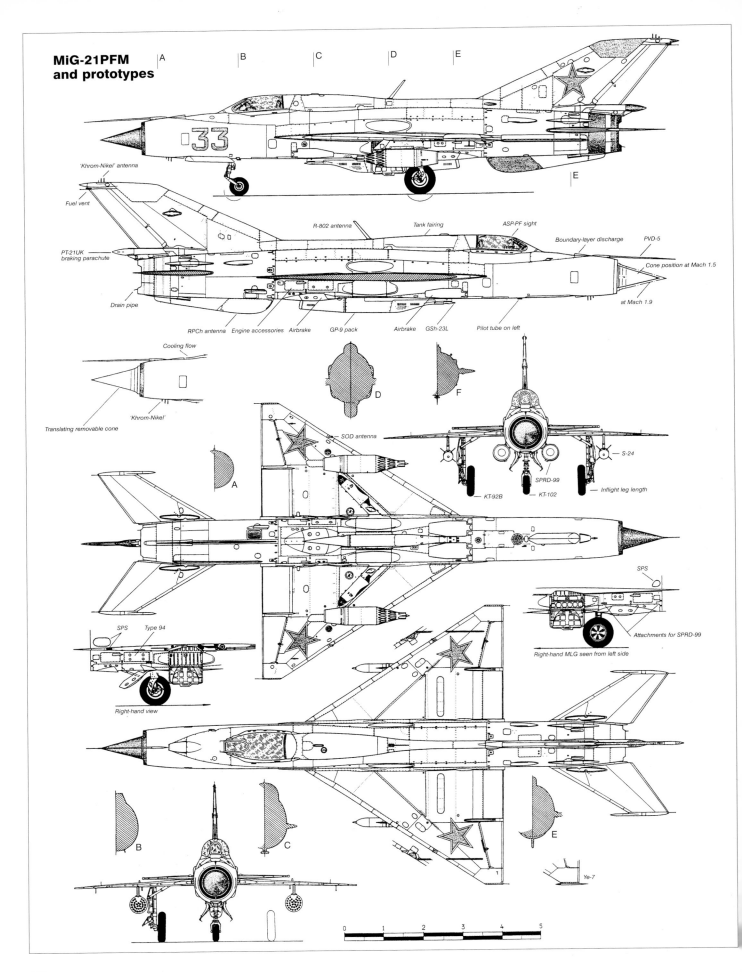

'Khrom-Nikel' antenna

Fuel vent

PT-21UK braking parachute

Drain pipe

RPCh antenna   Engine accessories   Airbrake   GP-9 pack   Airbrake   GSh-23L   Pilot tube on left

R-802 antenna   Tank fairing   ASP-PF sight   Boundary-layer discharge   PVD-5

Cone position at Mach 1.5

at Mach 1.9

Cooling flow

'Khrom-Nikel'

Translating removable cone

SOD antenna

S-24

SPRD-99

KT-92B   KT-102   Inflight leg length

SPS

Attachments for SPRD-99

Right-hand MLG seen from left side

SPS   Type 94

Right-hand view

Ye-7

0   1   2   3   4   5

130

MiG-21R

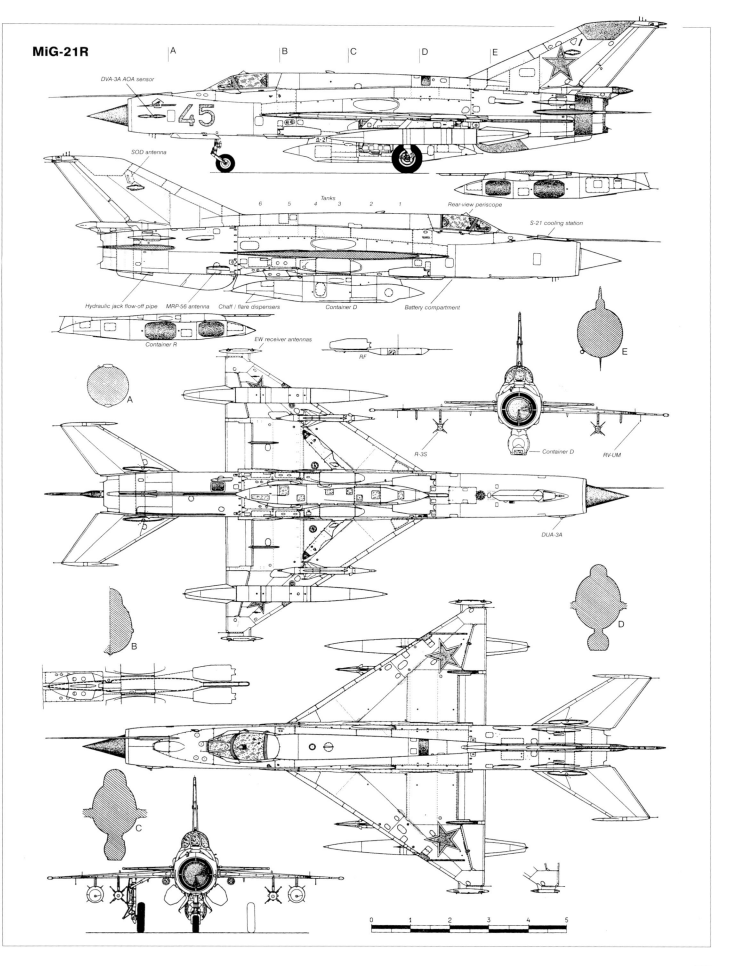

DVA-3A AOA sensor

SOD antenna

Tanks
6 5 4 3 2 1

Rear-view periscope

S-21 cooling station

Hydraulic jack flow-off pipe   MRP-56 antenna   Chaff / flare dispensers   Container D   Battery compartment

Container R

EW receiver antennas

RF

A

E

Container D

R-3S

RV-UM

DUA-3A

B

D

C

0   1   2   3   4   5

135

MiG-21bis

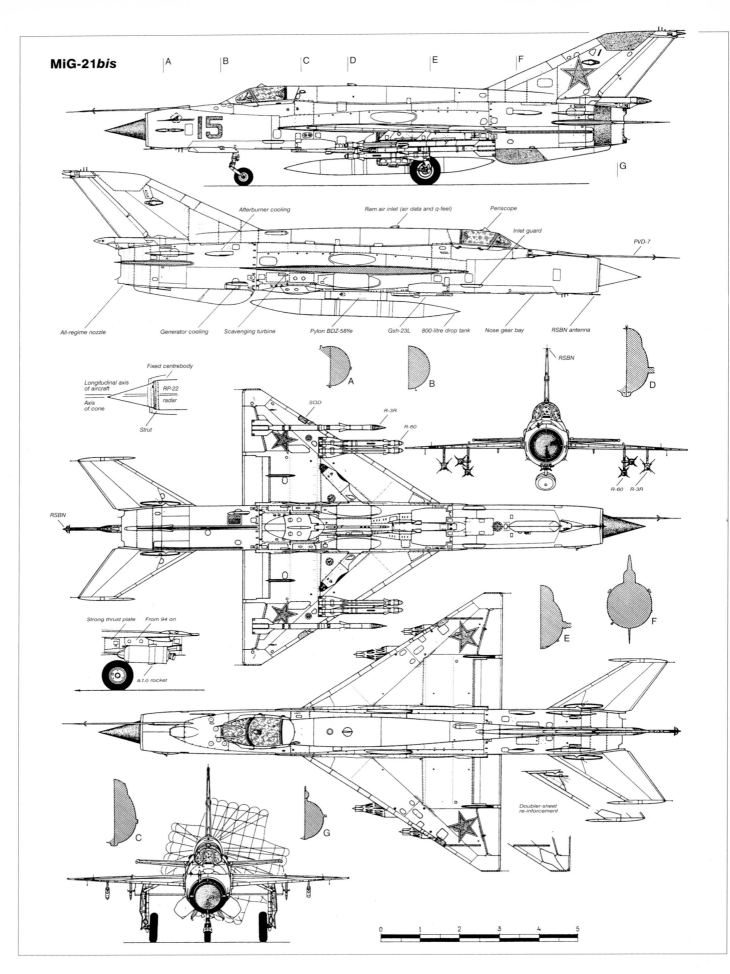

|A |B |C |D |E |F

15

G

Afterburner cooling   Ram air inlet (air data and q-feel)   Periscope

Inlet guard

PVD-7

All-regime nozzle   Generator cooling   Scavenging turbine   Pylon BDZ-58Ye   Gsh-23L   800-litre drop tank   Nose gear bay   RSBN antenna

A

B

D

Fixed centrebody

Longitudinal axis
of aircraft

RP-22
radar

Axis
of cone

Strut

RSBN

SOD

R-3R

R-60

RSBN

R-60   R-3R

E

F

RSBN

Strong thrust plate   From 94 on

a.t.o rocket

Doubler-sheet
re-inforcement

C

G

0   1   2   3   4   5

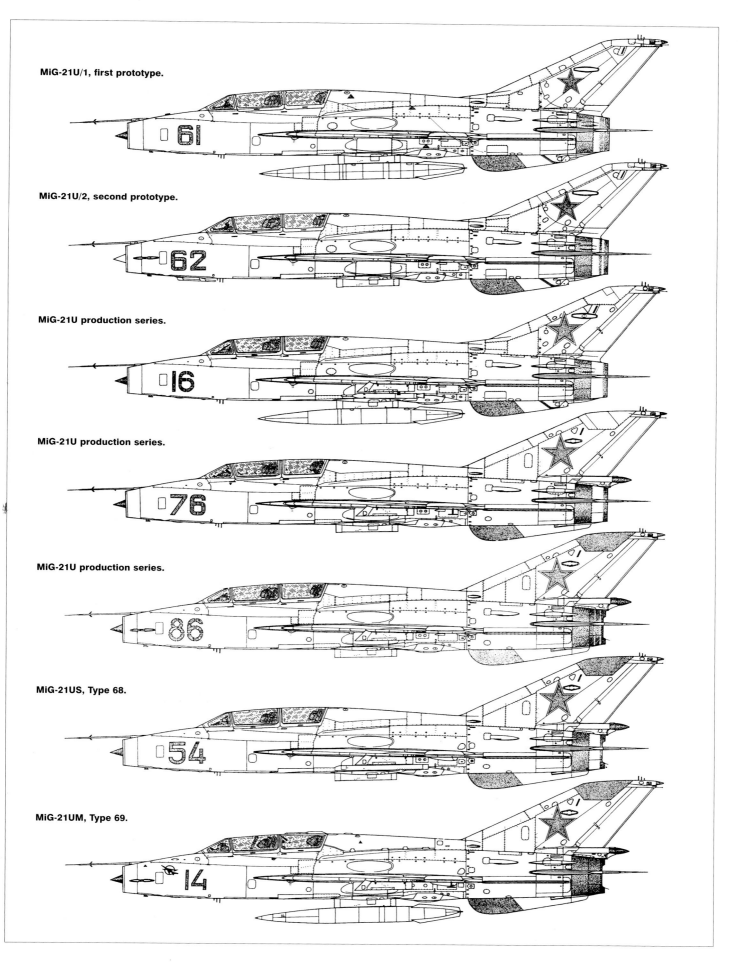

MiG-21U/1, first prototype.

MiG-21U/2, second prototype.

MiG-21U production series.

MiG-21U production series.

MiG-21U production series.

MiG-21US, Type 68.

MiG-21UM, Type 69.

MiG-21UM

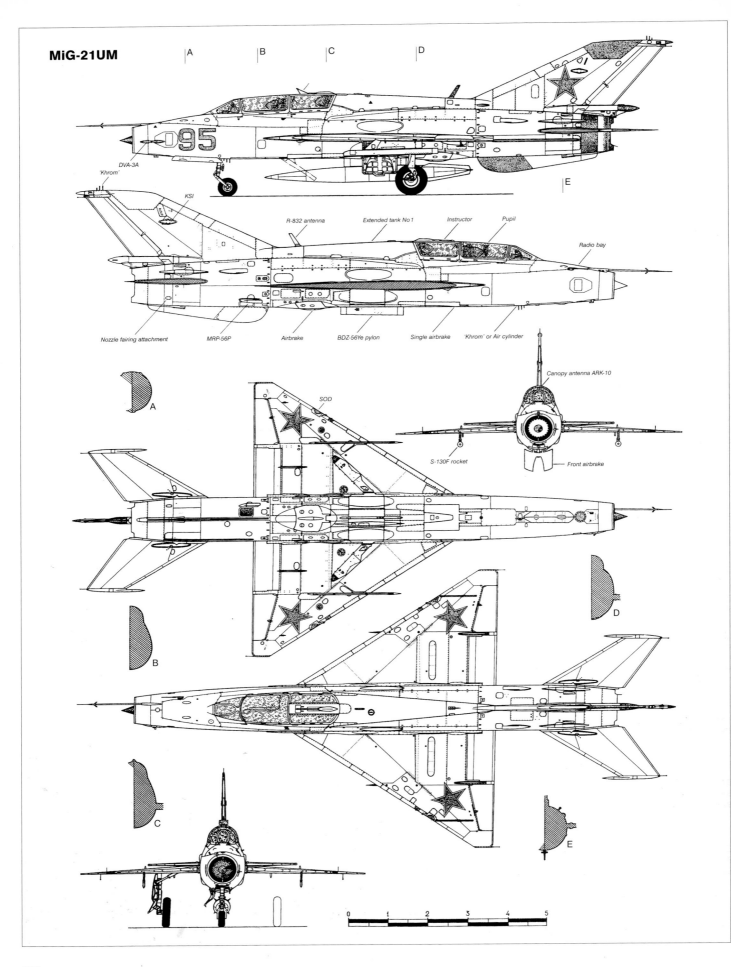

A   B   C   D

95

DVA-3A
'Khrom'

KSI

R-832 antenna

Extended tank No1

Instructor   Pupil

Radio bay

E

Nozzle fairing attachment   MRP-56P   Airbrake   BDZ-56Ye pylon   Single airbrake   'Khrom' or Air cylinder

A

SOD

Canopy antenna ARK-10

S-130F rocket

Front airbrake

B

D

C

E

0   1   2   3   4   5

MiG-21 Operators

The very nature of the MiG-21 and its many 'clients' militates against a really detailed listing of operators, the sub-types and quantities they have flown. Here an attempt has been made to show the wide sweep of users with sufficient data to convey the sort of operator they were, or are. After the country name comes the name of the air arm; MiG-21 types employed; maximum strength thought achieved; example(s) of individual aircraft with serial number and sub-type, where known; page references relating to illustration(s); for the USSR and Russia references are widespread and not itemised; status, current numbers operated etc, plus further notes. Readers will already have appreciated how fluid the situation is and will therefore appreciate that this listing is but a 'snapshot' in the lifetime of a phenomenal aircraft.

AFGHANISTAN
Afghanistan Army Air Force
Afghan Hauai Quvah

Types	F-13, MF, *bis*, U, UM
Max strength	70+
Examples	957 *bis*, 578 U
See pages	119, 127
Status	Perhaps 30-40

ALBANIA
Albanian People's Army Air Force

Types	F-7A
Max strength	20?
Example	0208 F-7A
Status	Thought current.

ALGERIA
Algerian Air Force
Al Quwwat al-Jawwiya Al Jaza'eriya

Types	F-13, M, *bis*, UM
Max strength	120+ ?
Examples	FA89 *bis*, FE209 UM
Status	Perhaps 36 current.

ANGOLA
Angolan People's Air Force
Força Aérea Populare de Angola

Types	M, MF, *bis*, U, UM
Max strength	80+
Examples	C326, C340 MFs
See pages	85, Rear cover
Status	30-45 current

AZERBAIJAN (formerly part of the USSR)
Azerbaijan Air Force

Types	?
Max strength	10?
Status	'Below 10' reported operational 1994.

BANGLADESH
Bangladesh Air Force
Bangladesh Biman Bahini

Types	MF, U, F-7M
Max strength	14, unknown number of F-7Ms (perhaps 20)
Examples	7201 MF, 046 UM, 1422 F-7M
See pages	56, 121
Status	Perhaps half of the MiG-built examples current.

BELARUS (formerly part of the USSR)
Republic of Belarus Air Force VVS

Types	??
Max strength	??
Status	Air force established 1992. Reported one regiment of MiG-21s.

BOSNIAN SERBIA
Bosnian Serbia Air Force

Types	RF
Max strength	?
Example	326 RF
See page	51
Status	Unknown.

BULGARIA
Bulgarian Air Defence Force
Bulgarski Vozdusny Vojski

Types	F-13, M, PF, PFM, R, *bis*, U, UM
Max strength	130 ?
Examples	027 F-13, 345 *bis*
See pages	68
Status	Updating remaining (102?) 1996-97?

BURKINA FASO (formerly Upper Volta)
Burkina Faso Air Force
Force Aérienne de Burkina Faso

Type	MF
Max strength	8-12
Status	All withdrawn.

CAMBODIA (formerly Kampuchea)
Cambodian Army Air Force

Types	*bis*, UM
Max strength	40
Examples	7110, 7121 *bis*, 7114 UM
See page	120
Status	Reported 16 *bis* and one UM extant 1994. Upgrades underway at IAI Lahav, for 10-20 – see Chapter 13.

CHINA
Air Force of the People's Liberation Army
Chung-kuo Shen Min Tai-Fang-Tsun Pu-Tai

Types	F-13, J-7, JJ-7
Max strength	750-950? (J-8 'Finback' 200?)
Examples	3147 J-7 II, 402 J-7 III
See pages	36, Chapter 11.
Status	400 J-7 (+100 with Navy), 50 JJ-7

CONGO
Congo Air Force – *Force Aérienne Congolaise*

Type	MF, U
Max strength	18?
Example	TN259
Status	Perhaps 11 plus 6 U, unknown if operational. Delivered 1986

CROATIA
Republic of Croatia Air Force
Hrvatske Zracne Snage

Type	MF, RF, *bis*, UM
Max strength	24 ?
Example	101 MF
Status	Independent from June 1991. Numbers quoted in 1994 by Republic of Serbia Krajina in complaint to UN. Some certainly ex Yugoslav Air Force. Others ex? About 18 operational 1995.

CUBA
Cuban Air Force - *Fuerza Aérea Revolucionaria*

Types	F-13, M, MF, PFM, *bis*, U, UM
Max strength	174
Examples	660 F-13, 377 MF, 368 PFM
See page	126
Status	150 thought operational.

CZECHOSLOVAKIA
& CZECH REPUBLIC
Czechoslovakian Air Force
Cesk Letectvo

Types	F-13, MF, PF, PFM, R, SM, U, UM, US
Max strength	about 450
Examples	0711 F-13, 7705 MF, 0310 PF, 4404 PFM, 1502, 2133 R, 7711 SM, 3756 UM, 0732 US
See pages	33, 37, 51, 53, 68, 118, 127
Status	Republic thought to have had about 150 at max strength, inc MF, R, UM and Ut. By mid-1994 this was down to a declared 80 with the intent of bringing this down to 40 by the end of 1996. Possible upgrade programme was announced for the remaining aircraft in late 1994 but thought now moribund?

Cambodian MiG-21*bis* line-up. Cambodian AF via
A J Walg – Aero Mapho archive

EAST GERMANY
East German Air Force – *Luftstreitkräfte*
Types	F-13, MF, PF, PFM, R, SMT, *bis*, U, UM
Max strength	240+
Examples	639 F-13, 709 PFM, 517 SMT, 963 *bis*, 215 UM
See pages	34, 54, 116, 125
Status	United with West Germany on 3rd October 1990 – which see.

EGYPT
Arab Republic of Egypt Air Force
Al Quwwat al-Jawwia Ilmisriya
Types	F-13, M, MF, PFM, PFS, R, UM, US, F-7B
Max strength	145+ (F-7B 80?)
Examples	8226, 8611 MFs, 613, 5207 PFMs, 8075 PFS, 8502 R, 5644 US.
See pages	42, 49, 55, 56, 119, 126
Status	Soviet-built examples were thought not, current. Spares deal with HAL of India late 1995 indicates otherwise.

ETHIOPIA
Ethiopian Air Force – *Ye Ityiopia Ayer Hayl*
Types	M, PF, *bis*, UM
Max strength	90+
Examples	1103 *bis*, 1012 UM
Status	60? Many in disrepair or stored.

FINLAND
Finnish Air Force – *Ilmavoimat*
Types	F-13, *bis*, U, UM
Max strength	61
Examples	MG-33 F-13, MG-116 *bis*, MK-103 U
See pages	34, 61, 125, 128
Status	24. Replacement with McDonnell Douglas F-18C/D Hornets underway,

GERMANY
German Air Force – *Luftwaffe*
Types	MF, PFM, PFS, *bis*, U, UM, US
Max strength	
Examples	23+17 MF, 23+15 PFM, 23+85 UM
See pages	67, 116, 126, 127
Status	In all 251 MiG-21s taken on. All retired. See East Germany entry.

GUINEA REPUBLIC
Guinea Air Force – *Force Aérienne de Guinée*
Types	??
Max strength	7
Status	Unknown, 5 thought withdrawn.

GUINEA-BISSAU (formerly Portuguese Guinea)
Guinea-Bissau Air Force
Force Aérienne de Guinea-Bissau
Types	??
Max strength	around 10
Status	Unknown, 6 (?) thought operational.

HUNGARY
Hungarian National Air Defence Group
Magyar Honvédség Repülo
Types	F-13, MF, PF, PFM, *bis*, U, UM
Max strength	120
Examples	902 F-13, 509 PF, 1844 *bis*, 1418 U, 907 UM
See page	57
Status	Upgrade programme announced 1992 for up to 50 *bis*, but not carried through. Hungary actively courting SAAB/BAe over the JAS.39X Gripen.

INDIA
Indian Air Force – *Bharatiya Vayu Sena*
Types	F-13, FL, M, PFM, *bis*, U, UM

Max strength	657+
Examples	BC873 F-13, C992 FL, C1496 MF, C2200 *bis*, U666 U.
See pages	34, 35, 43, 44, 55, 62, 121, 126
Status	380-390. Upgrade programme announced in late 1995 for about 120 examples, reportedly the *bis* fleet. It is unclear if this work will be done by HAL or through MiG-MAPO at the 'Sokol' plant (previously *Znamya Truda*, GAZ 30). Certainly MiG-MAPO are to act as design authority. During 1995 10 MiG-21UMs were acquired from Bulgarian and Hungarian air force stocks to act as attrition 'top-ups' with further examples possible.

INDONESIA
Indonesian Air Force
Tentara Nasional Indonesia-Angkatan Udara
Type	F-13
Max strength	20
Example	2164
See pages	125
Status	All withdrawn, mid-1960s.

IRAN
Islamic Republic of Iran Air Force
Type	F-7M
Max strength	up to 36
Status	Assumed operational, 20 with the Republican Guard.

IRAQ
Iraqi Air Force
Al Quwwat al-Jawwiya al-Iraqiya
Types	F-13, MF, PFM, U
Max strength	80+ (F-7B 75+)
Example	628 F
See pages	36, 125
Status	Unknown.

Above: **Rare image of Ethiopian Air Force MiG-21UM** Neil Lewis

Left: **Loading an ejector seat into Czechoslovakia's modified MiG-21U test-bed.** Yefim Gordon archive

Below left: **MiG-21F-13 MG-35 of the Finnish Air Force.** Yefim Gordon archive

Below: **MiG21*bis* of the Air Force of the People's Liberation Army, Laos. Note up-turned radome covers.** Lao AF via A J Walg – Aero Mapho archive

LAOS
Air Force of the People's Liberation Army
Types	F-13, MF, PF, *bis*, U
Max strength	44
Example	18 MF
See page	120
Status	20, plus 6 U.

LIBYA
Libyan Arab Jamahiriyah Air Force
Al Quwwat al-Jawwiya al-Libiyya
Types	MF, U
Max strength	94?
Examples	308 MF?, 218 U
Status	All thought withdrawn.

MALAGASY (Madagascar)
Malagasy Air Force – *Armée de l'Air Malgache*
Types	FL
Max strength	8
Status	Current?

MALI
Republic of Mali Air Force
Force Aérienne de la Republique du Mali
Types	?, U
Max strength	10?
Status	Thought withdrawn.

MONGOLIA
Air Force of the Mongolian People's Republic
Types	MF, PFM, U?
Max strength	12+
See page	120
Status	All withdrawn *circa* 1993.

MOZAMBIQUE
Mozambique Air Force
Forca Aerea Moçambique
Types	MF, PFM
Max strength	48+
Examples	06, 11 MFs
Status	Perhaps 25.

MYANMA (previously Burma)
Air Force of Myanma – *Tamdaw Lay*
Type	F-7M, FT-7
Max strength	36
Status	Deliveries began 1990.

NIGERIA
Nigerian Air Force
Types	MF, U
Max strength	33
Examples	NAF 661, NAF 674 MFs
Status	Perhaps only half now operational.

NORTH KOREA
Korean People's Army Air Force
Types	F-13, PF, PFM, U, UM
Max strength	180+
Examples	216, 218 PFMs
Status	135+, 30 U.

PAKISTAN
Pakistan Air Force – *Pakistan Fiza'ya*
Types	F-7P, F-7TP
Max strength	95
See page	121
Examples	88-509 F-7, 89-602 F-7TP
Status	Deliveries began 1991.

POLAND
Polish Air Force – *Polskie Wojska Lotnicze*
Types	F-13, M, MF, PF, PFM, RF, SMT, U
Max strength	385+
Examples	2223 F-13, 2007 PF, 6510, 8011 MFs, 5614 PFM, 2213 RF, 6510 UM.
See pages	33, 49, 52, 117, 126
Status	140 operational?

ROMANIA
Romanian Air Force – *Fortele Aeriene ale Republicii Socialiste România*
Types	F-13, FL, MF, PF, U
Max strength	150
Examples	4713 FL, 1120 U
See pages	118, 128
Status	Upgrades with Elbit, Israel, for 100 aircraft, underway (see Chapter 13).

Distinctive with their roundels on the tailfin, a pair of Aero L-29 Delfins shield a line-up of five Nigerian Air Force MiG-21MFs. via A J Walg – Aero Mapho archive

Impressive line-up of North Korean MiG-21PFMs. via A J Walg – Aero Mapho archive

RUSSIA – CIS
Air Forces of Russia
Voyenno-Vozdushnyye Sily
Types	MF, PF, RF, SMB, *bis*, U, UM
Max strength	400?
Examples	42 PFM, 411 R, 004 R, 204 UM
Status	Thought withdrawn from frontline service. Many late series examples still in use for fighter training, etc. Also M-21 drone conversion programme (see Chapter 13). Some CIS states (eg Kazakhstan) 'inherited' MiG-21s but have not operated them.

SLOVAKIA
Slovakian Air Force
Types	F-13, MF, PF, R, UM
Max strength	70?
Example	9904 F-13, 7714 MF
See page	56, 118
Status	60+. 'Top-ups' from Aero Vodochody, Czech Republic, reported late 1993.

SOMALIA
Somalian Aeronautical Corps
Dayuuradaha Xoogga Dalka Somaliyeed
Types	MF, UM
Max strength	10
Examples	224 MF, 208 UM
See page	119
Status	All grounded, wrecked during civil war. Chinese F-7Ms also quoted: unlikely.

SOVIET UNION
Air Force of the Soviet Union
Sovietskaya Voyenno-Vozdushnyye Sily
Types	F-13, MF, PF, PFM, RF, SM, SMB, SMT, ST, *bis*, U, UM
Max strength	1,200+
Examples	22 PFM, 23 SM, 05 SMT, 22 *bis*, 66 U, 204 US
Status	The USSR was dissolved in December 1991. 12 republics within: Armenia; Azerbaijan*; Belarus*; Georgia; Kazakhstan; Kyrgyzstan; Moldavia; Russia*; Tajakistan; Turkmenistan; Ukraine*; Uzbekistan. Those marked * known to have an independent air force (with MiG-21s) operational - *qv*. See under Russia – CIS.

SRI LANKA
Sri Lankan Air Force
Type	F-7BS, JJ-7
Max strength	6
See pages	Front cover, 121
Example	CF708 F-7BS, CTF703 JJ-7
Status	5 current.

SUDAN
Sudanese Air Force
Silakh al-Jawwiya as-Sudaniya
Types	MF, PF, U, F-7M
Max strength	18+ (F-7M unknown)
See page	119
Example	344 PF
Status	Unknown.

SYRIA
Syrian Arab Air Force
Al Quwwat al-Jawwiya al Arabiya as-Souriya
Types	MF, PFM, *bis*, U, UM
Max strength	250+
Example	1082 PFM
Status	120? Negotiating supply of spares from HAL of India late 1995.

141

TANZANIA
Tanaznian People's Defence Force Air Wing
Jeshi la Wanachi la Tanzania
Type	F-7A
Max strength	16
Status	Perhaps 13 operational.

UGANDA
Uganda Army Air Force
Type	MF
Max strength	12
Example	U-916
Status	Survivors (5) stored or derelict.

UKRAINE (formerly part of the USSR)
Ukrainian Air Force
Types	SM, *bis*, U
Max strength	195
Example	121 SM, 01 *bis*
See pages	62, 66
Status	Survivors stored or scrapped.

VIETNAM
Vietnamese People's Army Air Force
Types	PF-V, PFM, MF, *bis*, UM
Max strength	200+
Example	4326 PF-V, 5067 PFM, 5121 MF, 5205 *bis*, 8127 UM
See pages	45, 126, 128
Status	150?

YEMEN .
Air Force of Yemen
(North and South, countries merged 1990)
Types	M, PF, *bis*
Max strength	70+
Status	All withdrawn?

YUGOSLAVIA AND YUGOSLAV REPUBLIC
Yugoslavian Air Force
Jugoslovensko Ratno Vazduhoplovstvo
Types	F-13, M, PFM, R, *bis*
Max strength	220
Examples	22502 F-13, 25128 MF, 210 *bis*
See page	127
Status	About 100 thought on strength up to split of the country.

ZAMBIA
Zambian Air Force and Air Defence Command
Type	MF, U
Max strength	18
Example	AF 824
Status	15?

ZIMBAWE
Air Force of Zimbabwe
Type	F-7B or 'M, JJ-7
Max strength	48
Status	14?

Notes:

Jordan is reported to have received early F-7Bs and F-7Ms – unconfirmed.

Slovenia was reported to have had 'small stocks' of MiG-21s in mid-1993, but this is also unconfirmed.

Israel (page 83, 125) has also operated at least one example.

United States (page 36) is known to have evaluated and operated a 'small' combat training unit from Nellis AFB.

Top: **Night time shot of a Yugoslav MiG-21MF. Note the large cover for the PVD boom.**
Yefim Gordon archive

Middle: **A poor shot, but illustrations of Ugandan MiG-21MFs are very rare. Carnage around an MF, almost certainly at Entebbe.** via A J Walg – Aero Mapho archive

Above: **A fate that has befallen many MiG-21s in recent years. The remains of East German examples at Neubrandenburg, in November 1990, a month after German unification.**
Russian Aviation Research Trust

OKB SUKHOI

Vladimir Antonov, Yefim Gordon, Nikolai Gordyukov, Vladimir Yakovlev & Vyacheslav Zenkin, with Jay Miller

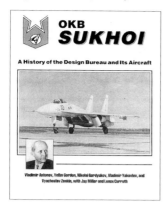

Another famous Soviet aircraft design bureau is thoroughly documented in this book, which is being prepared with the co-operation of the Sukhoi bureau, and with extensive access to their records and photo files. A huge amount of unpublished information, illustration and drawings is included on this important military aircraft designer. Each aircraft type is reviewed in detail, including prototypes, testbeds and projects.
Due for publication 1996 (3rd qtr)

Hardback, 280 x 216 mm, 296pp
1,000 photos/illusts incl 25 in colour
1 85780 012 5 **£29.95/US $49.95**

OKB MiG
A history of the design bureau and its aircraft

Piotr Butowski, Jay Miller

Beginning with a comprehensive overview of Soviet military aviation, the text methodically moves from the births of Mikoyan and Gurevich through to the founding of the MiG design bureau during 1939, its war years, and the period of greatest importance, beginning with the advent of the MiG-15 and the Korean War and continuing via the MiG-17, -19, -21, -23, -25 and -27 to the MiG-29 and MiG-31 era. A highly acclaimed work.

Hardback, 280 x 216 mm, 248pp
800 photographs, over 100 drawings
0 904597 80 6 **£24.95/US $39.95**

LOCKHEED MARTIN'S SKUNK WORKS
The First Fifty Years (Revised Edition)

Jay Miller

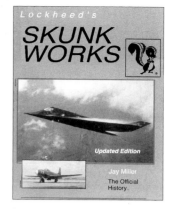

An updated edition of the 1994 original 'Lockheed's Skunk Works' written with the total co-operation of Lockheed Martin's Advanced Development Company. In a major 'pulling back' of the veil of secrecy, official histories of such products as the U-2, A-12, D-21, SR-71, and F-117 are finally brought to light.

This is the closest thing yet to a definitive history of this most enigmatic aircraft design and production facility.

Softback, 305 x 229 mm, 216 pages
479 b/w and 28 colour photos
1 85780 037 0 **£19.95/US $29.95**

We hope you enjoyed this book . . .

Aerofax and Midland Publishing titles are carefully edited and designed by a knowledgeable and enthusiastic team of specialists, with many years experience.

Further titles are in the course of preparation but we would welcome ideas on what you would like to see.

In addition, our associate company, Midland Counties Publications, offers an exceptionally wide range of aviation, spaceflight, astronomy, military, naval and transport books and videos for sale by mail-order around the world. For a copy of the appropriate catalogue, or to order further copies of this book, and any of the titles mentioned on this page, please write, telephone or fax to:

Midland Counties Publications
Unit 3 Maizefield,
Hinckley, Leics, LE10 1YF, England

Tel: (+44) 01455 233 747
Fax: (+44) 01455 233 737

US distribution by Specialty Press – see page 2.

Aerofax
YAKOVLEV'S V/STOL FIGHTERS

John Fricker and Piotr Butowski

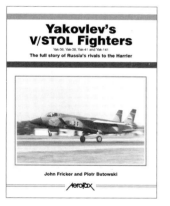

The story of Russia's programme to achieve a supersonic VTOL jet fighter can now be told, from the earliest experiments through to the astonishing 'Freehand' and on to the agreement between Yakovlev and Lockheed Martin to help produce JAST, the USA's next generation tactical fighter.

Using material never before seen in the West, this book tells the story of a programme that has to an extent, until recently, been shrouded in secrecy.

Softback, 280 x 216 mm, 44 pages
90 b/w photos, diagrams etc
1 85780 041 9 **£7.95/US $12.95**

Aerofax
LOCKHEED MARTIN F-117 NIGHTHAWK (Revised Edition)

Jay Miller

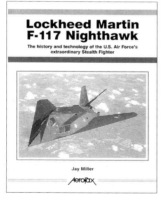

No aircraft has captured the public imagination in recent years more than the Lockheed F-117 'Nighthawk' - popularly known as the Stealth Fighter - first because of the immense secrecy and speculation during its development at the secret Groom Lake site in the Nevada Desert, and then because of its apparently spectacular success in the Gulf War. This is a much modified, updated and improved edition of an 'Aerofax Extra' last published in 1991.

Softback, 280 x 216 mm, 48 pages
106 b/w and 23 col photos, diagrams
1 85780 038 9 **£7.95/US $12.95**

Aerofax
NORTHROP B-2 SPIRIT (Revised Edition)

Jay Miller

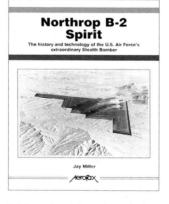

In this newly and thoroughly revised book, and using many detail photographs, the reader is taken through the complex process of assembling the B-2, the world of low-observable structures and systems that make up stealth technology, on to flight trials (including air-to-air refuelling with KC-10s) and service introduction. Full colour illustrations of the B-2's flight deck will enthral as will close-ups of many elements of this unique bomber.

Softback, 280 x 216 mm, 40 pages
100 b/w and 10 col photos, diagrams
1 85780 039 7 **£7.95/US $12.95**

Aerofax
TUPOLEV Tu-95/Tu-142 BEAR

Yefim Gordon and Vladimir Rigmant

During the 'Cold War' Tupolev's Tu-95 'Bear' strategic bomber provided an awesome spectacle. It was the mainstay of the USSR's strike force, a reliable and adaptable weapons platform. Additional roles included electronic/photographic reconnaissance and maritime patrol, AEW and command and control. The author has had unparalleled access to the Tupolev OKB archives, taking the lid off a story previously full of speculation.
Due for publication 1996 (3rd qtr)

Softback, 280 x 216 mm, c80 pages
c160 b/w and colour photos, diagrams
1 85780 046 X **c£11.95/US c$19.95**

Index

In order to make the index as easy to use as possible, references to oft-quoted items such as MiG OKB, VVS etc have been omitted. References to prototype and sub-type MiG-21s start with the chapter (Ch) in which they are dealt with in depth, then follows other pages in which they are mentioned in the narrative.

In cases where designations have been used twice (or more times), eg MiG-21I, this is not noted in the index.

Aero Vodochody S-106   31
Aero Vodochody L-29 Delfin   65
Aero Vodochody L-39 Albatros   65, 91
Aerostar (IAR)   91
Ageyev, A I   80
Belosvyet, AA   90
Belyakov, R A   22, 32, 77, 87, 90
Boeing B-52   85, 86
Bogorodskii, A P   16
Brunov, A G   22
Budkevich, S   90
Burtsev, F I   11
CAC/MiG-MAPO FC-1   80, 89
CAHI (TsAGI)   8, 9, 10, 11, 25, 34, 43, 70
CATIC Super-7   80, 90
Chengdu F-7 (also Airguard and Skybolt)   Ch 11, 90
Chengdu FT-7   Ch 11
Chengdu J-5 and JJ-5   77
Chengdu J-6 and JJ-6   77, 85, 86
Chengdu J-7   Ch 11, 32
Chengdu J-8   Ch 11
Dassault Mystère   82
Dassault Mirage F1   94
Dassault Mirage III   7, 81, 82, 84
Dassault Mirage 2000   60
Douglas A-4   85, 91
Dushkin, L S and KB   17, 20, 33
English Electric Lightning   7
Fedotov, A V   34, 35, 72
Gavrilov, V   54
General Dynamics F-16   60, 84, 89
General Dynamics F-111   85
Gorkii (GAZ 21)   12, 16, 20, 22, 25, 29, 37, 41, 44, 45, 49, 50, 57, 60, 88
Gudkov, O V   76
Guryevich, M I   7, 73
HAL Ajeet (Gnat)   92
HAL LCA   89
HAL Marut   81

Hawker Hunter   81
Hindustan Aeronautics (HAL)   45, 55, 60
IAI Kfir   84
Ilyushin Il-28   47
Klimov, V Y and KB   7
Kokkinaki, K K   22, 24
Kolesov, P A and KB   74
Korovin, N A   19
Kozlov, M   76
Krasilshchikov, P   11
Kravtsov, I M   41, 69
Lavochin OKB   8
Lavochin La-250   8
LII-MAP/-VVS, Zhukovskii   12, 16, 18, 21, 34, 43, 76
Lockheed F-104   6, 81, 82
Lockheed-Boeing F-22   89
Lyul'ka, A M and KB   7, 8, 12
M-21 (MiG)   46, 90
Makhalin, V S   16
McDonnell Douglas F-4   84, 85, 86, 91
McDonnell Douglas F-15   84, 86
MiG-AT and ATTA   88
MiG-MAPO   88, 90, 92, 93
MiG I-1   11
MiG I-270 ('J')   17
MiG SM-1   7
MiG-15   5, 7, 40, 65, 81
MiG-17   7, 8, 29, 40, 77, 84, 85, 86
MiG-19   7, 8, 9, 10, 11, 20, 24, 29, 40, 47, 77, 82, 83
MiG-21bis   Ch 8, 70, 91, 92, 93
MiG-21F   Ch 4, Ch 5, 37, 78, 81
MiG-21FL   Ch 6
MiG-21I   Ch 10, Ch 13
MiG-21M   Ch 7
MiG-21MF   Ch 7, 60, 79, 91, 92
MiG-21MT   Ch 8
'MiG-21PD' (23-31)   34, 73
MiG-21PF   Ch 6, 31, 33, 48, 90
MiG-21PFM   Ch 6, 50, 74, 90
MiG-21PFS   Ch 6
MiG-21PF-V   Ch 6, 84
MiG-21R   Ch 7, 41
MiG-21RF   Ch 7
MiG-21S   Ch 7, 74
MiG-21SM   Ch 7
MiG-21SMT   Ch 8
MiG-21ST   Ch 8
MiG-21U   Ch 9, 44, 79
MiG-21Ye   45, 90

MiG-21-93 (MiG-MAPO)   Ch 13
MiG-21-200 (IAI)   Ch 13
MiG-23   12, 16, 19, 20, 34, 70, 71, 74, 89
MiG-25   37, 39
MiG-29   60, 88, 93
MiG-31   37, 88
MiG-33   80, 89
MiG-110   88
Mikoyan, A I   7, 12, 73, 76, 87, 88
Mikulin, A A and KB   7, 8, 9
Minayev, A V   10
Moscow (GAZ 155)   7, 24, 38, 71
Mosolov, G K   11, 34, 71
Mukhin, V G   18
NAMC A-5   90
NAMC J-12   78
Nefyedov, V A   14, 21
NII-VVS, Akhtubinsk   8, 19
North American A-5   86
North American F-86   5, 6, 81, 82
Northrop F-5   85, 91
Nyenartovich KB   40
Orlov, V A   70, 74
Ostapenko   40, 74
Prokhanova, N   67
Rolls-Royce Nene   7
SAAB Gripen   89
Saunders-Roe SR.53   17
Saunders-Roe SR.177   7, 17, 20
Savitskaya, S   68
Sedov, G A   12, 14
Shenyang   77
SOKO Novi Avion   89
Solovyeva, M   43
Sukhoi, P and OKB   7, 8, 16
Sukhoi S-1   12, 16
Sukhoi Su-7   8, 16, 35
Sukhoi Su-9   8, 37, 39
Sukhoi Su-11   8, 39
Sukhoi Su-15   37, 39
Sukhoi Su-17   7
Sukhoi Su-20   84
Sukhoi T-3   16
Sukhoi T-43   20
Tbilisi (GAZ 31)   12, 16, 60, 67, 68
Tsybin, P V and OKB   47
Tsybin RSR   47
Tumanskii S P and KB   7, 8, 9, 14, 16, 20, 26, 71
Tupolev, A N and OKB   76
Tupolev Tu-128   37, 39
Tupolve Tu-144   74, 76
Valdenberg, M R   87
Vasin, V P   18
Volk, I   76
Volkov, F F and KB   50, 70
Vought F-8   81
Yakovlev OKB   8
Yakovlev Yak-27   20, 47
Yakovlev Yak-28   37, 39
Yakovlev Yak-140   8
Ye-1 (MiG)   8, 9, 17
Ye-2 (MiG)   Ch 2, 17, 19, 21
Ye-4 (MiG)   Ch 2, 9, 21
Ye-5 (MiG)   10, 12, 14, 16, 19, 21, 69
Ye-6 (MiG)   Ch 3, Ch 5, Ch 9, 9, 25, 29, 30, 32, 34, 71
Ye-7 (MiG)   Ch 6, 48, 50, 71
Ye-8 (MiG)   Ch 10, 35, 48
'Ye-33' (MiG)   67
Ye-50 (MiG)   Ch 3, 10, 12, 16
'Ye-66' (MiG)   24, 32, 43, 67
'Ye-76' (MiG)   43
Ye-152 (MiG)   70
Ye-155 (MiG)   34
'Ye-266' (MiG)   34
Yelyan, E   76
Zaitseva, L   43, 67
Znamya Truda (GAZ 30), Moscow   22, 31, 43, 54, 57, 60, 67